PRAISE FOR
WINNING PICKLᴇBALL

"Dave Satka helps the reader understand the importance of practice, how to focus on the present and his advice on how to increase your pickleball IQ are spot on. This book can help all players improve their game!"

—**Moira Roush**, eight-time US Open Pickleball Champion

"In college, Dave Satka was the kind of player any coach would want. Although not a gifted athlete, Dave's hard work, dedication, passion, and endless practice propelled him to become a key player on a Division I-level team. Dave has applied that same work ethic to pickleball to become a highly accomplished, respected player, as well as a Certified Instructor and Ambassador for the game. His sheer determination to be the best mentally prepared player on the court comes through loud and clear in this inspiring book. Are you determined to improve? Help has arrived with *Winning Pickleball*. Read and learn!"

—**Doug Rowe**, former Head Men's Tennis Coach and D-1 Player, USPTA Professional

WINNING PICKLEBALL

WINNING PICKLEBALL

EXPERT STRATEGIES FOR

NEXT LEVEL PLAY

DAVID SATKA

Foreword by Leigh Waters & Anna Leigh Waters,

#1 Ranked Pickleball Champions

Hatherleigh Press is committed to preserving and protecting the natural resources of the earth. Environmentally responsible and sustainable practices are embraced within the company's mission statement.

Visit us at www.hatherleighpress.com.

WINNING PICKLEBALL

Library of Congress Cataloging-in-Publication Data is available upon request.
ISBN: 978-1-57826-995-2

Cover Design by Carolyn Kasper

Printed in the United States
10 9 8 7 6 5 4 3 2 1

To my son,
Benjamin

▶ CONTENTS

▶ FOREWORD
BY LEIGH WATERS &
ANNA LEIGH WATERS

*Leigh Waters and Anna Leigh Waters (self-dubbed as "Team Waters")
are professional pickleball players and a former #1 ranked doubles
team. The only mother-daughter team in professional pickleball, they
were featured in the first nationally televised pickleball match in
history on CBS Sports. In 2019, Anna Leigh became the youngest
professional pickleball player in history and as of early 2024, she is
ranked #1 in the world for singles, doubles and mixed doubles by the
Professional Pickleball Association. Leigh, a former NCAA Division I
tennis player at the University of South Carolina, supports Anna Leigh
as her coach.*

Who would have thought a sport with a funny name like pickleball
could make such a difference in so many people's lives?

We were introduced to pickleball by my father (Anna Leigh's grandfa-
ther) in 2017 in Pennsylvania, and it changed our lives forever. We were
immediately hooked on the game and spent the next year playing as often
as possible. We played indoors on gym floors; outdoors on lined tennis
courts; we played with folks of all ages, all athletic abilities, and all levels.
Little did we know that the sport we started playing for fun would soon
become a full-time passion — and a full-time profession.

Anna Leigh and I quickly became known as a mother/daughter dynamic
duo, taking the pro game by storm. By 2019, we had won major titles and
finished the year as the #1 professional women's team. Fast forward to the

present: Anna Leigh is currently World #1 in singles, mixed doubles, *and* women's doubles, while I work as her coach, all while coaching a handful of other pros and serving as an advisor to pickleball companies.

If you are reading this book, you too are likely hooked on the fastest growing sport in America. You too love what pickleball has to offer—the fun, the camaraderie, the health benefits, the competition!

And sure, you likely want to improve your game. But not everyone wants to be a pro or put in the time necessary to be the best of the best. This book will do just that: it will give you tips to improve quickly, as well as tell stories, make you laugh, and give you insights into how the pros play and think. You will even get to learn from a Team Waters mishap where the daughter was the wiser of the two Waters!

Pickleball has brought so much joy to so many, and we know it will continue to do so for many more generations to come. So, from Anna Leigh and me to you, enjoy the book, get out there, keep playing, have fun, and we'll see you on the courts!

—Leigh and Anna Leigh Waters, "Team Waters"

▶ INTRODUCTION

This book is an attempt to empty my brain of 45 years of tennis, pickleball, and athletic experiences and share them with you. I want you to enjoy learning how to become a better pickleball player by profiting from my personal journey. Every personal story and anecdote is 100 percent true with no embellishments. I'm *not* a superstar professional pickleball player or an exceptionally gifted athlete. However, I *am* a pickleball nut just like you, dedicated and doing my best to realize all of my potential.

I am targeting players of any age between the 2.0 and 4.5 level of play. It is my goal to reach pickleball players that want to improve their play but may not be great athletes, have no prior tennis experience or are not athletically gifted in any way. You may have never played a sport in high school or have ever been coached in the proper techniques to become an athlete but somehow you became addicted to pickleball. Of the nearly 5 million pickleball players in the United States, a large percentage are being athletic for the first time! This is awesome! Americans need to get moving! I believe this is the primary reason why pickleball is the fastest growing sport in America.

The things I am about to tell you can be done immediately with little time, money or athletic ability. This is not a technical book. It will not go over the mechanics of strokes or shot making. There is no series of drills to follow. I will leave that to the hundreds of other books, videos and articles written about drills and strategy. The greatest thing about this book is that you can get significantly better without endless hours of practice or thousands of dollars of lessons. Pickleball is considered an "unsolved" sport. Meaning, there is no "correct" way to play. Strategies and shots are consistently evolving but the advice in this book will *never* change, it is fundamental to success at any level of pickleball.

HOW TO USE THIS BOOK

If you've just picked up this book with the intention to read it from cover to cover, great! I hope you enjoy it, but don't try to digest it all at once. It's intended to be savored like a five-course meal. Take one chapter at a time. It will take a while for your brain to fully grasp the many new concepts that I'm recommending for you to adopt. Once you're comfortable with the changes and have successfully implemented them into your routine or game, then move to the next chapter. Remember: *Improvements don't happen without a plan and all good things take time.*

First things first: Take some time to develop a measurable goal. What kind of player do you want to be? What would you like to achieve in pickleball? Visualize what peak performance looks and feels like for *you*. Here's my recommended action plan:

Step 1: Start a pickleball-specific fitness program.

Step 2: Develop your own personal readiness routine.

Step 3: Go shopping. Buy a new bag or fill your current bag with all the recommended equipment.

Step 4: Think about how you can become a more-focused player.

Step 5: Consider ways to increase your pickleball IQ.

Step 6: Make a conscious effort to become a mentally tougher player.

Step 7: *Think* how you can progress just by improving court positioning, footwork, and shot selection.

Step 8: *Think* how you can be a better partner.

Step 9: Make a plan to start practicing or practicing more often.

Step 10: Challenge yourself and celebrate improvement!

This book is the perfect complement for players planning to take lessons. Pickleball instructors do not have time to talk about most of the topics addressed in these pages. They know you are paying for court time and that you expect to be hitting balls. Let this book handle the *mental* aspects of the game while your instructor deals with the physical mechanics of the game. Pickleball instructors would do well to supplement your on court lessons by assigning specific chapters of this book for you to read *off* the court.

I am positive this book can help all players to some degree excluding professionals. Successful professional pickleball players know the difference between winning and losing for them is a very fine line. They know that no stone can be unturned to give themselves even the slightest edge to enable them to bring home the gold! They are experts at all the things you are about to read. Each of the following chapters will break down the many facets that comprise what I call the "Winner's Edge." Some of it is easier said than done but all of it is very "doable." So, let's get started!

> "I believe wisdom is wasted on the old, all you can do is part
> with it but very few will take it."
> —Raymond Reddington, *The Blacklist*

▶ CHAPTER 1

LEVELS OF PLAY, YOUR CONFIDENCE & YOUR GOALS

This chapter and the rest of this book will cover many facets of pickleball that are rarely discussed but can easily improve your game. Understanding levels of play, having confidence in your game, and establishing clear goals are three important topics I chose to discuss first. These three topics and all the remaining subjects covered in this book require little or no athletic ability to implement. It is my hope that explaining these concepts through my life story as an athlete, former tennis player and pickleball player will make learning these concepts a little more entertaining.

GAUGING YOUR SKILL

Since I was a young boy, I have been trying to answer the question: How good am I at whatever sport I might be playing? This process first started when my neighborhood pals would pick teams for our games. You immediately knew where you stood among your peers by how many boys were picked ahead of you. Soon, my playmates would begin to recognize specific skills in others. It became assumed I would play quarterback when we played football. John was always the punter. Donny was a running back, Jerry a wide receiver, Lenny a defensive back, and so on. Boys with no particular skills were told to, "Stay in and block." This became the initial basis of my confidence as a young athlete.

In high school, I relished the opportunity to play summer recreation games with varsity athletes from surrounding schools, where I learned even more about my skill level and my deficiencies. When I heard where the best high school players were practicing, getting on the same court with them became my top priority. My friend Lenny and I would jump into my 1974 Chevy Monte Carlo and rush to Valparaiso High School to get a shot at playing against one of the best basketball players in the state, Roger Harden. Roger would later be crowned Mr. Basketball (best player) in Indiana and go on to play at the University of Kentucky, a national basketball power. He is now a member of the Indiana Basketball Hall of Fame.

In my mid-30s, I was still playing basketball twice a week and wanted to see how good a professional basketball player really was. I had no aspirations for myself, but I still wanted to challenge my skills and gain a complete understanding of the levels of the game. Amazingly, I got to play with two of the Chicago Bull's World Championship team, Stacy King and BJ Armstrong. Both were working out in a suburban Chicago gym when I happened to be visiting the city. I recall telling Stacy to get in the post so I could feed him the ball. He replied, "No man, I don't wanna hurt anybody." He was 6'11", 240 pounds! I had never played with anyone this big and so talented. Stacy was right. He would have hurt anyone trying to guard him. Both Stacy and BJ were working on the weakest parts of their games, not their strengths. I was privileged to experience their pro basketball skills.

I also had the honor of guarding another professional. Doug West is a legend from Altoona, PA. When I encountered him, he was a seasoned NBA player for the Minnesota Timberwolves and often matched up against Michael Jordan. As the tallest man on my summer recreation team, I was man-on-man with Doug in a league game. I remember setting a back pick on him, trying to free one of my teammates for a shot. Doug unintentionally knocked me down just by extending his arm to my chest as he felt his way around me. That was the first time I was ever knocked down when expecting contact. He was the most amazing athlete I ever competed against. He was extremely powerful. He could run like a deer and jump to touch the top of the backboard. He even competed in the

NBA's slam-dunk competition one year. Doug was *at least* ten times the athlete I was, with ten times the basketball skills I had. This experience was a sobering reality for me and made me take stock of my athletic ability, which, by comparison, was pathetic.

I learned a great deal playing with these great athletes. They all had three things in common: an incredible work ethic, laser focus, and an aura of absolute confidence. Nothing distracted them. If they missed a shot or made some other kind of mistake, they immediately and instinctively moved to their next position on court. Their belief in themselves was absolute. *These points are crucial for maximizing your pickleball potential.* You must believe you are the best player on the court. Stay in the "zone," the here and now. Sure, you'll make mistakes, but stay focused on the *next* shot, not the previous one.

On the tennis court, I had the same drive to experience the next level of competition. In the beginning, I decided to play tennis just as a way to get out of school early. I showed up at tryouts with my father's T-2000 aluminum racquet, the kind Jimmy Connors made famous. I enjoyed hanging out with my new teammates and somehow had some success at the junior varsity level. My pride soared and so did my confidence because it was rare for a freshman to play any sport at this level. Maybe I *was* a good athlete, I thought. My early tennis success inspired me to begin practicing seriously.

I was fortunate to have a coach who was a true tennis junkie. I put in many hours of trial-and-error practice and asked a ton of questions anytime I met or played against a really good, more experienced player. New pickleball players should be asking lots of questions just as I did.

"Hard work always beats talent when talent doesn't work hard."
—Tim Notke, high school basketball coach

TO GET BETTER, LEARN FROM BETTER

As a high school senior, I was thrilled to receive some letters of interest to play college tennis at the Division III level, but I wanted to attend Indiana State University (ISU) in Terre Haute since they had one of the finest criminology programs in the country. However, I was unaware that my father had written to ISU's men's tennis team coach and, as a result, that got me an invitation to try out. I trained hard all summer and showed up for the first day of tryouts ready to go. There were players from all over the state trying out and the varsity players were all nationally or regionally ranked, it was a challenging moment. I worked hard during drills and showed an aggressive intensity against my match-ups. The coach liked my attitude and work ethic and saw my potential. I made the cut and walked on to a Division I tennis team! What an opportunity!

I had access to college-level training facilities, great practice partners, and professional coaching for the first time, benefitting from all the rigorous training regimens, not to mention hitting thousands of tennis balls. I began practicing with varsity players who were far above my level and struggled to keep pace but continued to hang in there and grind away at fundamentals. I posed many questions to my new teammates, such as how they hit certain shots, when they used them, and which strategies worked best. Soon, I began to hold my own with the varsity players and my confidence grew to where I thought, "Hey, maybe I *can* play with these guys!"

Talking to pickleball players who are much better than you are is a very smart thing to do. It compliments them to be asked how they do certain things on the court, how they prepare, or what they did to get to their level. Most players will be happy to answer. Better players in your club *want* to help, because your improvement will provide them with more competition. The best player to ask is the one who just beat you in a tournament. Ask them what you need to do to get better or what their strategy was to beat you. It's a rare opportunity to discover the truth about your game. Jack Nicholson, in the movie *A Few Good Men*, could have been talking about pickleball players when he famously proclaimed, "You can't handle the truth!" No friend or club member is likely to risk offending you because they know you Your best chance of learning the truth about your game can most likely come from a superior opponent, so set aside your pride and be "coachable." The truth will sting a bit, but the benefits can be pure gold.

I found out that making a Division I (DI) team and *competing* at that level are two different things. Indiana State is within a three-hour drive to several Big Ten schools, Notre Dame, and many great Kentucky schools. I struggled mightily with this level of competition, going from dominating in high school to being dominated in college. It wasn't until the conference tournament my second year that I finally realized my potential by defeating a #1 seed 7-6, 7-6. This was my first experience of "peak performance" (see Chapter 2) in college and what a perfect time for it. I was "in the zone." My focus (see Chapter 5) was locked in. I had tunnel vision, which allowed me to see the ball more clearly and seemed to slow the speed of the game. My strokes felt smooth, and every shot felt crisp, hit in the sweet spot of my racquet. I felt powerful but completely relaxed. My body knew how to execute the shots and my brain allowed them to work, despite the adrenaline surging inside my muscles. Most importantly, though, I finally *believed* that I could win. Belief is a key factor for becoming a successful pickleball player.

> "I believe in, 'Believe.'"
> — Ted Lasso

The thrill of competition, taste of victory, and great satisfaction of performing at my peak spurred me on. I made it my goal to become a winning college player from this point on. My third year saw significant improvement, but it wasn't until senior season that I realized that it was the *mental* side of the game (see Chapter 6) holding me back from reaching my goals. I had all the shots and enough weapons to win but I had neglected the mental aspect of my game. I failed to reflect on how my opponents responded to my game and how I should have adjusted to their games. I was only concerned with playing *my* game and blamed losses on poor technical or physical execution. Consequently, I learned to self-evaluate much better and adapted my game for each opponent.

Thus, I became a complete player, and it resulted in my first and only winning season. I achieved my goal and found my maximum level of play in the process. Peak performance lies within everyone, but the challenge is finding it.

GOALS: SETTING AND ACHIEVING

Pickleball players need to set goals if they want to get better and win more. As I have told high school students for years, "Reaching goals doesn't just happen; you have to make a plan and follow it." Students don't get into Harvard just because they want to. I know many pickleball players who complain about their game or say that they want to play at a higher level, but they have no plan to accomplish it. It reminds me of former students who said they wanted to be a veterinarian someday but who weren't even taking advanced classes. By the way, "hoping" to become a 4.0 player isn't a plan. I find that most players stop improving after their first year of playing. Most play at the same level year after year when they should be surprised how much better their game is when compared to the past year. When I look back at my past years' game, I say to myself, "Wow, I actually thought I was good in 2018!"

My friends who know about my tennis career are surprised when I say that I love pickleball more than tennis. I explain to them that there are more great tennis aspects in pickleball, such as extended rallies, clever stratagems, and fast-paced exchanges among all four doubles players. These "bang-bang" exchanges may happen once in three sets of tennis but they happen once every few minutes in pickleball. An amazing around-the-pole (ATP) shot may only happen once or twice in a tennis career but it happens every few hours in pickleball. I also tell them that I never had a chance to experience tennis at the professional level as I have with pickleball. It feels great to finally compete in a sport at the highest level. Pickleball allowed me to fulfill my quest to fully understand levels of play. Playing one professional tournament, though, hasn't fulfilled my ultimate goal in pickleball. I still have hopes — *and plans* — to re-enter that level again.

Many of you are probably frustrated with a few players in your club who don't properly self-evaluate their game. These are the players who seem to be oblivious to losing. How can someone lose nine games in a row with nine different partners and not try to understand why? They typically make lame excuses and go on their way, completely unaware of the impact their poor play has on their group's level of play and fun. Because pickleball is so easy to play, lesser players can "hang" with superior players for a brief time, unlike in the sport of tennis. The moment a lesser player walks on a tennis court with a superior player they know it. Tennis requires much more athleticism and sheer power. There might be a 100-mph serve barreling across the net! This doesn't happen in pickleball and, as a result, creates an opportunity for lower-skill players to dilute the enjoyment of a more-accomplished group. This is why you need to make an honest appraisal of your current skill level and support that with some empirical evidence, such as winning the majority of your games, assuming you have an equally matched partner. The result will be confidence to relax and play your best, because you have nothing to prove. Unless you live in a pickleball hotbed, you'll need to seek out better players to get the necessary feedback.

I credit a great deal of my confidence to fellow USAPA Ambassador, Peter Popovich. I never met Peter or knew of any of the Ambassadors before I attended the national conference at Club Med in Port St. Lucie, Florida. I soon learned that Peter had won multiple gold medals at several national tournaments, playing at the 4.5-5.0 level. Many amazing players were there, and I enjoyed a ton of great play. I was unsure of my level back then and lacked confidence. When asked, I told people that I was a 4.0 player. Finally, Peter approached me and told me to stop calling myself a 4.0 because I was definitely a 4.5. *That* made my day! His compliment gave me a great shot of confidence since I did not have to impress anyone anymore. As a result, I relaxed and played much better.

During my athletic life, I have enjoyed very high levels of any sport I played and reset my goals accordingly. I have won my share of medals and trophies, but I have found that playing to my "peak performance" level (see Chapter 2) is the most satisfying. I experience almost the same feeling, regardless of winning or losing, if I have played to my peak. I recall one of the first times I was "in the zone" and performed at my peak but lost the tennis match. I was confused as to how I should feel. I felt guilty for not helping the team to win but proud to have played my best. I was concerned that my happiness might be misinterpreted by my teammates. Fortunately, my teammates all understood and even congratulated me. Isn't playing your best really what we strive to do, all we *can* do?

Another great way to learn how to be a better athlete is to simply observe some great ones. The quarterback for the New York Jets told reporters about how much he watches and tries to learn from Buffalo Bills quarterback, Josh Allen. Watching live sporting events is great fun and an excellent source of information. When I was younger, I became mesmerized watching great athletes compete. Instead of watching the drama of a close game, try to watch a specific player. Notice their fitness level, intensity, relaxation, focus, confidence, and footwork. Then realize their high level of play. These are the aspects that you can acquire as an amateur pickleball player. Someone once said, "If you can see greatness in others, then you already have greatness in yourself."

PLAYING UP AND PLAYING DOWN

You may be thinking, I have to do all of this just to play with my friends? Well, yes and no. *No*, if your friends are all at the same level and no one ever improves. *Yes*, if you want to keep playing with your group or be able to play with your friends in higher-level groups or play in tournaments. *Yes*, if you like winning! Remember: it's always appropriate to play *down* a level (play with 3.0s if you're a 3.5 or higher) but it's not appropriate to play *up* in a group above your level without an invitation. You never want to be the "wet blanket" or person who plays up for selfish reasons and ruins the fun for the higher-level players.

Long, fast-paced points filled with hard shots and great defense are what make pickleball fun. I nicknamed points that include at least two "resets" and a finish with a winning shot as a "Vlasic" (a great brand of pickles). My pickleball friends often hear me shout, "*Now* we are playing pickleball!" or "*That's* why I play pickleball!" whether I win or lose a "Vlasic" point. These points are only possible with four equally talented players. Everybody has days when they play poorly, but good players know the difference between a player off his or her game and a player who doesn't belong in this group. The point here is to "Stay in your lane" regarding your level of play. When you're winning 75 percent of your games at your current level, you may be ready to "level up." It's very important to have success at one level before moving to the next. Dominating at a certain level means that you have acquired the requisite skills necessary to advance and you have gained much confidence as well. People, however, are generally poor self-evaluators. We all tend to think we are better looking, smarter, or more fit than we really are. Pickleball players are no different. Very few players underestimate their playing level. If you don't have an official ranking and have any doubts about playing in a higher-level group, ask a member of that group about your skill level before showing up. Chances are that they've already noticed your fine play and will be happy to have you join in.

Sorting out levels of play is a struggle every growing pickleball club faces. My local club decided to let everyone "self-rate" and then a committee would make individual corrections as needed. The club's board provided International Pickleball Teaching Professional Association (IPTPA) Skill Level Assessment Sheets (available at iptpa.com/iptpa-rating-skills-assessment) to all members. It was a good plan, but one problem surfaced: 95 percent of club members refused to rate themselves. Why? We know many incorrectly assumed that they would be separated from their friends. Others might have been embarrassed to learn their true rating was far lower than what they told people. I believe the real reason is so that members could continue to play at any level they desired. Many believe that playing at a higher level provides some form of status and may allow them to brag about how many points they won against better players. I heard only one member tested themselves against the standards. Backhand shots are the most obvious separator between 3.0/ 3.5 and 4.0 levels. If a player is avoiding hitting any shot with his or her backhand, then they are usually no better than a 3.5. The backhand side might be slightly weaker for a 4.0 player, but at the 4.5 level, there is usually no difference between backhand and forehand shots. In fact, the backhand is often the stronger of the two shots at the 4.5+ level.

WHAT MATTERS IS PLAYING BETTER

All this consternation over levels of play is a distraction when, in fact, players should be thinking about how they can improve. It seems much easier to manipulate a rating than it is to actually improve. If you want to get better and need a good benchmark, then review the skill-level standards sheets mentioned above. These give specific numbers for the amount and types of shots needed to be hit for each level. You and a friend can test each other privately if you are unsure of your skills. For example, a 3.5-level player needs to be able to hit 8 out 10 shots into the kitchen from the middle of the court. A 3.0-level player only needs to be able to hit 5 out of 10. The ideal approach is to become better skilled than simply to play at whatever level you *think* you are.

My goal is to improve every time I step on the court, and this should be your goal, too. Of course, this is the point of practicing, but I also learn from recreational and tournament play. When I play recreationally, I have a specific goal for the day, such as, "I'm not going to hit an 'out' ball today," or, "I'm going to hit a drop on all my third shots today." I then reflect on these goals during my drive home. If the drive is after a defeat, I'll focus on the causes but try not to dwell on them. There is no better teacher than losing. Reflect on the causes for your loss and note if a pattern emerges. Always think about what went *right,* too. Even in defeat, there were likely some bright spots.

If you're driving home in victory, savor the memory of key points won and allow yourself to rejoice. Playing at my peak is my ultimate goal. That's more important than winning, to me. Of course, winning is great and playing at my peak makes that more likely to happen. Learning the nuances of the game is a big part of why I'm so intrigued by this game, but it's those fast-to-slow-to-fast action points (Vlasics) and my peak-play quest that feed my addiction. I want to dink, bang, and reset every point! I believe that a major difference between advanced and intermediate players is the amount of time each spends reflecting on their play. I regularly see players leaving a ladder-play session, after not winning a single game, without a care in the world. You will *never* see a good player do this. Reflecting and resetting goals must be a priority for any real improvement to take place.

The goals you choose to make need to be specific and measurable in order to make steady progress. Your long-term goal may be to win a tournament at a certain level. This goal can be measured with a gold medal. Short-term goals are the steppingstones to achieving a long-term goal. For example: Goal — Hit 20 drop shots in a row from the baseline into the kitchen. Goal — Hit 30 serves in a row into a specific half of the serving box. You might make a major change to the mechanics of a shot and the goal would be to stay with the changes for at least two months. It's important to realize that you always tend to get worse before you get better when you make a change in shot mechanics. Stay the course!

Short-term goals are great for recreational play, too. Make play with your regular group more interesting by making a specific short-term goal. For example, you can say to yourself, "I'm going to out-dink everyone today!" Balls that you normally try to speed up get dink'd, instead. Avoid lobbing on a particular day. Make playing a "clean" game your goal, that is, a game in which you made *zero* unforced errors. Making a shot that is easily attacked by your opponent is considered to be an error. Hitting winners has nothing to do with this goal. In fact, playing a clean game is a super goal for every game you play because chances are that you'll not ever lose any game that you play "cleanly."

From a psychological perspective, think of your chief long-term goal as being able to reach a level where you're playing *chess* instead of checkers on the pickleball court. Checkers is just hitting shots to certain locations and reacting to your opponent's shot. Pickleball becomes chess-like to advanced players when they create a strategic game plan and then use their skills to carry it out successfully. It's incredibly rewarding and loads of fun to play a sequence of shots as part of a plan that leads to easy put-away smashes and ultimate victory. *That's* how to play chess on a pickleball court. The rest of this book is devoted to helping you develop your plans to achieve your long-term goals.

> "A goal properly set is halfway reached."
>
> —Zig Ziglar

CHAPTER 2

UNDERSTANDING PEAK PERFORMANCE

The goal of this book is to show players of all levels how to improve their game through greater mental awareness. You don't have to be a natural athlete to become a better player; you just need to learn how to "add brain to your game." We all would like to be better players. Some of us may think improvement will happen by watching YouTube videos, taking lessons, or simply playing more often. All of these approaches can help to some extent, but not nearly as much as incorporating the techniques detailed in this book.

Playing more frequently will certainly help beginners, but more experienced players merely reinforce their bad habits by doing that, unless they are playing with a specific goal in mind. For those who say, "I just play for the exercise," or "I play for the social aspect of the game," I say, "*Poppycock!*" If this is the sole reason for playing, then why keep score? The next time you crush the "exercise" or "just-for-fun" player 11-2, comfort them by saying, "Well, at least you got your steps in!" or "Wasn't *that* fun?" See how much they like that! We keep score to *compete* and, even if they won't admit it, *everybody* likes to win! Winning is fun! I much prefer it to losing, don't you?

PLAYING TO WIN

Now that we're clear that the ultimate goal of playing pickleball is *to win*, how can you improve your chances of doing that? I'll discuss the importance of practice at the end of this book, but now I want you to focus on the *mental* side of maximizing your potential, something you can do right now to get better. When you maximize your potential and play your very best, professionals will say you exhibited "peak performance," or you played "in the zone." You might have heard it put another way, as, "I'm in the groove" or "I'm hot today." I prefer to say, particularly to my doubles partner, "You're like butter today — on a roll!" All this simply means that you're playing your best. In this chapter, I'll break down the elements that comprise peak performance. Most importantly, I'll explain why that happens and how you can make it happen more often. We all want to have a game like Michael Jordan did in the 1992 NBA finals, when he made six three-point shots in a row and had to shrug his shoulders in humble acknowledgement that, granted, he wasn't being fair to the other team.

Playing "in the zone" is a state of physical and psychological bliss. It's a period of time when you're completely relaxed, highly focused, and are executing your game seemingly without effort. It's a feeling of ecstasy for an athlete. I can recall being in the zone only a few times in my sports career. There were a few rare days, as a high school basketball player, when the basket seemed twice its normal size. I couldn't miss from any distance. The same is true for tennis, as I mentioned previously, when I had a few "in-the-zone" moments on the court. There even have been a few zone days for me in pickleball, too, when the game seemed magically easy. During all of these occasions, I wasn't aware of anything beyond the court. I had no sense of time or location; it was like having tunnel vision. Teammates were there, but I had no awareness of them. The Zone is difficult to reach, but I'll do my best to help *you* get there.

I was fortunate to have peak-performance training in college. During my first off season, Coach Rowe conducted multiple team sessions in a darkened room. He had us lie on the floor, get comfortable, and close our eyes. He wanted us to assume a meditative state of mind and told us to think about the best match we ever played, recalling as many details as possible about that day: our food intake, pre-match activities, weather during the match, and our physical and mental feedback. Once we had accumulated all those details, he told us to make a "mental movie" of that special day. My cinematic epic came from my senior year in high school.

It was a perfect, warm, sunny September day, a home match and I was playing on my favorite court, executing shot after shot effortlessly. Shots that I usually struggled with all went in. I felt like I could hit a coin placed anywhere on the court. I seemed to hit my racquet's sweet spot every shot, noting my opponent's look of surprise and eventual resignation. It was the best win of my tennis career up to that point and resulted in this comment in the newspaper from the opposing team's coach: "I think Dave Satka could have beaten anyone in the state today." That was the highest praise I've ever received in sports. Even my usually stoic Dad was more excited than I had ever seen him.

Coach Rowe finished our session by asking us to give our mental movie a title. One team member entitled his "Poetry in Motion." Coach was pleased with our titles until my Malaysian teammate, Rostam, said that his movie was called "Volunteers." Coach asked if he was talking about the movie starring Tom Hanks and John Candy. Rostam responded in deadpan seriousness, "Yes, *that's* the movie!" Coach just laughed, but in Rostam's defense, Coach Rowe may have failed to fully explain the art of visualization to our team's international players.

Having a complete understanding of visualization is at the heart of peak-performance training. The best way to understand how visualization can be an effective tool may come from the U.S. military operation to locate and neutralize Osama Bin Laden. You need to learn how exercising your imagination can help your pickleball.

Ten years after the September 11th terrorist attacks, American intelligence discovered that Bin Laden was hiding in a secure Pakistan compound. U.S. forces obtained detailed information about the compound's layout and defenses but had no intel about the building's interiors. Army Special Forces constructed a matching mock compound and Navy SEAL Team 6 practiced for months about exactly what each team member was to do the second their helicopter landed at the compound. The obvious question: How could they possibly train for what they needed to do once they entered an unmapped building? Answer: *Visualization.*

Each member made a personal "movie" of how they would enter and clear any type of room they encountered. They imagined what furniture might be in the room, the lighting, hiding places, other people in the room, and other variables. Once these mental scenarios were set, they rehearsed them in their minds hundreds of times, along with the "director's cut" variations to allow for potential contingencies. The result of all this painstaking effort was a surgically precise strike that "neutralized" Bin Laden. U.S. Special Forces are the most highly trained, capable, respected, and feared soldiers in the world, and for good reason.

The purpose of the incredibly difficult training to become a Navy SEAL or Army Green Beret is not only to ensure physical stamina but also to instill the mental toughness (see Chapter 7) and discipline necessary to complete the most difficult missions. These elite warriors are quick to note that *mental* challenges far outweigh physical conflict. For them, *visualizing peak performance* is a matter of life or death.

You don't have to be a Navy SEAL to think like one. *You can learn how to visualize success on a pickleball court.* If you can't see yourself winning the perfect point, how can you expect to do it? First, close your eyes and search your memory for the best match of pickleball you have ever played. Then, try to catalog as many elements as possible about the day you played that great match. This may take some time, but it's well worth documenting.

TAKE SOME NOTES:

- How did you prepare to play that day?
- What did you eat that day?
- What were you wearing when you played?
- How well rested were you before your match?
- What were the weather conditions?
- Where was your match played?
- What made you especially focused that day?
- How did you feel on the court and after the match?

Note anything that might have been different about that special day compared to other days you've played. Of course, it's much easier to do this immediately after playing your best. When I know a friend has played a particularly outstanding game, I'll tell him or her to take some notes of all the things I mentioned above, as soon as possible. Documenting a great day of pickleball with the adrenaline of winning in your blood is a good thing!

Next, try to visualize key game situations. Attempt to break down all the elements of outstanding point(s) you played.

FOR EXAMPLE:

- What type of serve did you hit?
- Where did it land?
- What type of third shot did you use?
- How did you advance to the non-volley line?
- Did you use good footwork?
- What did your ready position at the non-volley line look like?
- What was your fourth or fifth shot?
- Were you feeling aggressive or calm?
- How did you win the point?

Finally, piece all this information together to see yourself performing masterfully and *make your movie.*

Visualize and relive what peak performance looks and feels like! The goal is to try to replicate the variables that made you play great that day. If you can do that and go on to produce "sequels" to your movie, you'll be up for an ESPY before you know it. The night before your next match, visualize playing the perfect point when you are serving and another when you're receiving. Try this in complete silence, in your darkened bedroom, as you're about to drift off to sleep. Experts say the brain consolidates short-term memory during sleep. These are the memories that you want to take to the court the next day. This technique has proven to be effective for students facing exams and now is just as useful for pickleball players.

If you find that visualization works well for you, by all means keep using it as a tool for match preparation. Famous professional athletes have found that staying with a winning combination of pre-game prep can pay off handsomely. Hall of Fame baseball player, Wade Boggs, became known as "Chicken Man" due to his pre-game meal ritual. He started eating chicken early in his career because it was inexpensive, but when he batted four-for-four one game, he attributed his success to his preference for pre-game poultry. So, chicken became his eternal entree before every game for the duration of his stellar career. Boggs played 18 seasons, that's over 3000 chicken dinners! Part of Michael Jordan's peak-performance "movie" involved him wearing his "lucky" University of North Carolina shorts under his Chicago Bulls uniform. Rafael Nadal takes a teeth-chattering cold shower 45-minutes before every match! Tiger Woods always wears a red shirt when playing a Sunday final round. Each of these great players strongly believes that they need specific rituals in order to enable a peak performance.

If you want to create your first in-the-zone experience, it all starts with careful preparation. Let's assume that your game is in order. You can never achieve peak performance with a mechanical (shot execution) or physical (injury) issue plaguing your game. However, even fundamentally flawed players can reach and inhabit the zone to achieve peak performance. In fact, during the last tennis match of my college career, I was in the zone and lost! My peak performance was not good enough to take third place at the Missouri Valley Conference tournament. I was at complete peace with the loss because I played to my highest level. In other words, Simone "The Queen of Pickleball" Jardim's peak performance is going to be *way* better than your peak performance, but fear not. Just remember — playing *your* personal best *is* peak performance, regardless of the level of your play.

"Baseball is ninety percent mental. The other half is physical."

— Yogi Berra

CHAPTER 3

PEAK PERFORMANCE READINESS ROUTINE

Finding the "zone" and peak performance doesn't just happen. You have to work for it!

When preparing for a tournament, you may need to do most, if not all, of the things I'm about to discuss a day or two in advance of match play, especially if an 8:00 a.m. tourney check-in requires that you get up quite early. I allow for at least 90 minutes of morning prep before my first match, not including travel time to the tourney site.

This chapter details my six "Readiness Routine" steps. Rather than undertaking all six steps at once, I recommend adding one step at a time to your pre-match prep process. Take small bites, not one big gulp. Do as *M*A*S*H*'s Major Charles Emerson Winchester said: "I do one thing at a time; I do it very well; then I move on." Once you've established your readiness routine, use it for all levels of play, from friendly club play to tournaments. A familiar routine will not only assure that you're prepared, but it can also help to relieve pregame jitters and instill confidence. Most importantly, though, completing each of these steps will facilitate getting into the Zone and realizing peak performance.

If you perform these six steps before playing, you *will* improve. This routine is foolproof! In fact, I would say that it's virtually impossible *not* to be a better athlete and pickleball player if you follow *this* process:

STEP 1: FITNESS AND PEAK PERFORMANCE

Fitness can't be instantly acquired on game day. It's a critical component of your maximum potential that takes time and effort to develop. You don't have to be a great athlete to be in great shape. Fitness and good health go hand in hand. *Staying* in shape, however, is not easy and is a significant mental challenge. Maintaining the mental discipline to keep working out at the gym while avoiding overeating or drinking (partying) too much is a lifelong challenge. Just getting to the gym is often the hardest part of the workout. I know a former marathoner who told me that putting on his running shoes was the hardest part of his training runs.

Having a workout buddy with similar goals can be a big help with your motivation to stick to a schedule and get the most out of every workout session. Staying fit is a *lifestyle*, not something to feverishly seek before swimsuit season. Going on a "diet" doesn't result in long term fitness. What happens when the diet is over? Most people return to the same negative habits that caused the problem in the first place. I heard someone once say, "I have a balanced diet: a beer in each hand!" Sure, that's funny, but you need to make a personal commitment to *live* like an athlete in order to realize your true potential, which may shock you once you reach it.

One thing I immediately notice about all my opponents in tournaments is their level of fitness. I thought my fitness level would be an advantage, but instead, it was only just enough for me to keep pace. There are some amazingly fit senior pickleball players out there who have maximum agility, the strength to execute their shots, and the stamina to play multiple intense games, then recover quickly, and go at it again. This is the reward for taking your body's athletic needs seriously. This is the goal that I want to help you achieve, regardless of your age or skill level.

Fitness challenges become more difficult with age. Dr. Nathan LeBrasseur, of the Mayo Clinic's Center on Aging, notes, "We achieve peak muscle mass by our early 40s and have a progressive deterioration from that point on, resulting in as much as a 50 percent loss by the time we are in our 80s or 90s. Most of us will lose approximately 30 percent over our lifetime."

Despite that discouraging outlook, exercise can be the "Silver Bullet" to slow or reverse muscle loss. Pickleball can be part of that solution, but it is not enough. Strength training (weightlifting) more specifically addresses muscle loss and will help you be a better pickleball player. Most health insurance plans now cover a portion of gym membership fees. For those over 65, the Silver Sneakers program is a great deal. If you find a gym that also has pickleball facilities, you can realize a double benefit!

Since pickleball is less physically demanding than sports like tennis or racquetball, many pickleball players believe that fitness is not very important. Consequently, I believe that the seemingly moderate-to-low physical demands of pickleball are a significant reason for its explosive growth, especially among seniors. I once asked an older gentleman from Florida how much he plays. He chuckled, "Oh, not that much, just *twice* a day." This may be possible at lower skill levels but playing at the 4.0 level and above is much more demanding. A three-hour Advanced-play session will nearly exhaust even the fittest players. Points at this level are longer, often requiring bursts of speed and maximum intensity. Simply holding a ready position for longer periods of time can tax one's stamina. Most people don't realize that being physically fit increases their ability *and* confidence!

I learned about the connection between fitness and confidence as an Army ROTC cadet in college. The Army believes that their officers not only need to be able to physically lead by example but also to display the confidence that inspires soldiers to follow them. By the end of the advanced training course, in the rugged mountains of the Pacific Northwest at Fort Lewis, Washington, I was in the best shape of my life. Once I had reached maximum fitness, my commands became colored with authority and confidence. I felt like I could do anything! Being as fit as you can will help you execute better shots, increase your confidence on the court, and could become an intimidation weapon for your game.

The three elements of total fitness are: *flexibility, strength, and endurance.* I'll discuss more about flexibility in Step 3. There are hundreds of videos, books, and personal-trainer programs that can teach you about strength and endurance. Two of the foremost experts in performance training are Mark Verstegan and Michael Boyle, who have written top-rated books, which you could add to your library as supplemental resources.

The best fitness tip I can give you is to *concentrate on your weakness.* At the gym, it's not uncommon to see men (or even women) with "ripped" upper bodies working out *on their upper bodies!* When do these physical specimens ever hit the treadmill? I have a friend who played on my softball team. He could bench-press over 400 pounds, but he couldn't stretch to catch a sinking liner or run for an extra base without pulling a hamstring. Was he fit? Many thought he was *super* fit, however, he lacked two of the three fitness keys: flexibility and endurance.

Here are my pickleball-specific fitness tips. Due to the No-Volley Line (NVL) or, more commonly, "Kitchen line," you need to be extra fit in a couple key areas. The NVL prevents stepping forward, making it impossible to transfer your body force into the ball from your fixed back foot to your forward-moving foot. Therefore, the only way to generate power in this fixed-feet position is to twist or "coil" at the waist, just like throwing a frisbee. Thus, *core strength* is essential. I often work on my core muscles while waiting for my turn to play, and sometimes while watching television at home. I place my forearms on a towel and do repeated front/side "planks," which are terrific core strengtheners. Planks are much better than traditional sit-ups or leg lifts because they do not strain the neck or lower back. There are lots of variations on planks to keep things interesting. It's hard to find a fitness expert who doesn't recommend this exercise.

The need for lateral movement in pickleball and overall quickness puts a premium on leg strength. I run and do deep squats to work on my thigh strength. Upper-leg strength also helps me get into a better ready position and protects my lower back from too much waist bending at the kitchen line. I also jump rope as a pregame warmup or while I am waiting to return to play. Jumping rope is great for both cardio fitness and footwork (see Chapter 8). That's why all boxers jump rope. These simple exercises can be done anywhere, without cost or a gym.

Fitness can also delay the aging process or help you compensate for a disability. You may recall when Michael Jordan came out of retirement to play basketball for the Washington Wizards. He arrived with a huge upper body. During his career with the Chicago Bulls, he played "above the rim" and was known as "Air Jordan" and "His Royal Airness." His slender physique and incredible muscle definition were ideal for jumping around and over defenders. With the Wizards, though, he was much thicker, having realized that he could no longer jump like he did early in his career. So, he bulked up his upper body to gain separation from defenders. He reinvented himself to accommodate his aging and was still able to average 21 points per game at the age of 40.

Tiger Woods made a similar body change to overcome the disabilities he suffered from a terrible car crash, which shattered his leg and badly injured his back. Knowing that he could no longer use his lower body to generate power for his golf swing, he built up his upper body to compensate. Fourteen months later, he miraculously won the Masters! You must do an honest self-evaluation of your fitness level in order to maximize your potential. I recently heard a player say to her partner, "I just can't get to those lobs." In this case, an honest self-evaluation would have revealed her need to do some endurance training (treadmill or road running), which would also reward her with increased leg strength, quickness, and weight loss. Of course, *motivation* is the key factor. I wondered how badly she really wanted to get to those lobs and how she would feel once she could.

STEP 2: NUTRITION AND SLEEP

Nutrition and proper rest are essential for general health and for gaining a winning edge prior to that big day on the pickleball court, whether during club play or in a tournament. I try to eat a high-carbohydrate, "carb-load" dinner the night before a tournament. Carbs give the body energy and will help fight off fatigue. A spaghetti dinner or something with potatoes is my preference. Any time I'm scheduled to play in the morning, my pregame meal is always oatmeal with blueberries, a banana, and nuts. Oatmeal is loaded with vitamins and minerals and offers another small carb-load.

It also seems to ward off hunger long enough to get me through the morning session of a tournament. Bananas are another great source of energy and, because of their potassium, they can help to prevent leg cramps on a hot day during a long, intense match.

Sleep is another energy booster that many take for granted. Think about how great you feel when you get an extra hour or so of shuteye on the weekend. Plan to go to bed early to get that extra hour (or two) of game-changing sleep when pickleball is on the morning horizon. Wake up energized and eager to play!

STEP 3: STRETCHING

Stretching is essential for being an effective, competitive athlete. It pre-pares the muscles — *and mind* — to prepare for action. Flexibility is often overlooked as one of the three key components of total fitness. Rarely do I see anyone stretching prior to a workout at my health club or prior to playing pickleball. I recently participated in a tournament where the doors to the facility's main building were locked early that morning and didn't open until 30 minutes before play was to begin. Dozens of players left their cars and immediately began warming up on court. Only *three* people began by stretching.

Pickleball demands the body to make pivots, lunges, twists, and a variety of bending movements, which puts a strain on muscles and joints. Doctors and physical therapists these days report a huge increase in joint-related injuries, especially among seniors, since the massive surge of pickleball play began across America. Flexibility that comes from an effective stretching routine will help to prevent injury and improve your play. For example, a player with good flexibility will be able to bend down into position to make a shot, using his/her legs, knees, and trunk, rather than simply reaching with an arm, losing the power needed to make the return.

The best types of stretches to use *prior* to play are called *dynamic*. This is a form of stretching that involves movement, such as trunk twists, walk-ing lunges, and leg swings. Search YouTube for "Dynamic Stretches" to see the proper techniques for these. Stretching becomes even more important with aging. Muscles and tendons lose their elasticity as we get older. There is a 69-year-old woman in my local group who stretches *before and after* every play session. She is so limber that many of us think of her as a contortionist! She is never injured, can easily handle all the bending required in pickleball, and recovers quickly. At the other extreme, Ben Johns hires a physical therapist to accompany him to every tournament. This therapist conducts four sessions with Ben on each day of competition. The sessions consist of a multitude of therapies including dynamic and static stretching.

STEP 4: WARMING UP

Pickleball players are ridiculously bad at this! Every sport I have ever played included executing all game-related movements *prior* to playing. Have you ever seen a tennis player start playing without hitting every shot, or a basketball team fail to run a lay-up line and shoot around? In baseball, they even have a special place called the "bullpen" for pitchers to warm up before entering the game, and they will warm up again before every inning. All this is done before an extended stretching session in the locker room that no one sees. Pickleball players consider walking from their car to the courts as their warmup! They will hit a few dinks and then want to start play immediately. Somehow, this became the pickleball warmup norm everywhere. How can anyone expect his or her body to perform well without a proper warmup?

Serious athletes *always* stretch and warm up before they play. Probably the best thing you can do is jog around the court a few times or jump rope for 60 seconds. Better yet, if weather permits, ride your bicycle to the courts! Bottom line: Do at least *something* to get your blood flowing and muscles warm. Ideally, get a light sweat going before play begins. Try to hit every type of shot at least a few times before starting. If time doesn't permit, then do a volley-volley drill (no bounces!) from the kitchen line. This will heighten your reflexes and energy level for fast-paced pickleball. If you can do only one thing to warm up before a match, don't dink! Dinking is the absolute worst thing you can do, yet that's what most players do.

A good warm up can play a role in increased confidence. John, a very fine, young, but cocky player (4.5 level) showed up late for a play session recently. He walked from his car to the courts, hit a couple of dinks, and announced, "I'm ready!" He then hit his usually hard first serve into the bottom of the net. He went on to lose that first game badly. He probably assumed that his first game would warm him up and, after that, he would return to playing at his normal-level next game. You know what they say about "assuming."

John's next game was against two excellent players (one of whom was me!). John was now in a situation where he had to play his best or face losing again. He tried to turn his game up a notch but continued to miss routine shots, most notably the one shot over which he had full control: his serve. I didn't do an exact count, but I estimate that John missed nearly a dozen serves during our two hours of play. This was a perfect example of how the lack of a proper warm up can lead to poor play and a loss of confidence. Near the end of our play, John was hitting soft little bloop serves, just to get them in. He lost many more games than he normally should have that day. Note that this happened to a man who is a 4.5 player with two decades of prior tennis experience. It can happen to you, too.

Regardless of what sport I ever played, whenever I had a great pregame warmup, my confidence was sky-high and I would often say to myself, "I'm gonna play great today!" Some of my basketball teammates once called me the best warmup player in the league. That may sound like high praise, but I can assure you, it was no compliment!

STEP 5: HYDRATION

Hydrating before, during, and after pickleball is not only important to replace fluids but it's also key for injury prevention, aerobic capacity, energy level, muscle endurance, and recovery. Water accounts for 70 percent of body weight, about 10-12 gallons' worth! Some experts call water the "Elixir of Life." The average adult needs 8-10 glasses a day. There's nothing more crucial for an athlete's body than water. NFL great, Tom Brady, drinks 2.3 gallons of water per day and twice that when he exercises. Granted, this is extreme, but it emphasizes the importance of hydration. Note that sports drinks like Gatorade are only necessary if sweating is profuse. These drinks replace depleted electrolytes and are helpful in restoring some carbohydrates, but water is still the best for all-around hydration.

If you're going to drink more water, why not drink the best? The purist water is steam-distilled and filtered. Tap water contains trace amounts of contaminants that can't be removed by your local water treatment plant. Water there gets processed with chlorine and fluoride is usually added. There's no way to know the number of pollutants that may exist in the pipes that transport water to your home. Well water quality varies by location since water tables can absorb various unhealthy elements. Bottled water is not much better than tap water. I use a tabletop distilling system from Waterwise Purification Systems that removes volatile organic compounds (VOCs) and 99 percent of all impurities. It makes one gallon of pure water in about four hours, and it tastes great.

STEP 6: MENTAL PREP

Pre-match mental prep may be the toughest of these six steps. It's amazing how much our brains control us subconsciously. Try to recall the times your brain refused to let you sleep or demanded that you sleep longer. Can you set your brain to act as an alarm clock? The night before a tournament, my brain is like a 12-year-old child's on Christmas Eve, when sleep becomes a real problem for me and my bladder adds a lot of steps to my Fitbit count. How about the times you pulled an all-nighter in college, or when your brain pushed your body to its physical limits? Consciously or subconsciously, your brain is Command Central and far more powerful than you probably realize, even during the relatively mild stresses of a casual game of pickleball. Anticipate the games your mind will play and plan accordingly.

During my pre-match prep, if I know who I'll be playing, I'll think about a specific plan of attack for this individual or team. If I'm playing in a tournament doubles match, I'll think about how to highlight my partner's strengths and ways to cover his/her weaknesses, plus what tactics I want to employ, based on how I've been playing lately.

For years, researchers have confirmed the power of music with respect to various forms of mental health. Music has been proven to improve focus and relaxation. I like to use music as a distraction for my pre-match anxiety and to pump up my adrenaline. Music stimulates my motivation and enthusiasm but also fires up my confidence and positivity. I don't know any players who go to the trouble to get psyched up using their favorite music and then feel like they're going to lose! Some prefer soothing music to calm their nerves; others power up to classical music like Tchaikovsky's *1812 Overture*. I prefer hard-driving classic rock-and-roll. REO Speedwagon's "Roll with the Changes" or Rush's "Tom Sawyer." "Eye of the Tiger" by Survivor, "Don't Stop Believin'" by Journey, and "Start Me Up" by The Rolling Stones are on my playlist, too. It's all about finding your ideal level of intensity. Music can be a powerful ally. Never underestimate the power of positivity. Believe in yourself and your game. Expect to win if you've done all the right prep. Maybe playing "We Are the Champions" by Queen will propel you to the top of the medal stand!

POST-GAME ROUTINE

STRETCH

Stretching after you play gives your body and mind a chance to gradually wind down. It also reduces the amount of lactic acid in your muscles that can generate soreness if left untended. Stretching will also limit muscle and joint strain. The best types of stretches for this purpose are called *static*. These are the ones most people know. They involve holding a single position for 20-30 seconds while carefully stretching muscles to their maximum. Once again, a quick YouTube search will provide you with examples and proper techniques. The main benefit of a post-game stretching routine is a quicker recovery and a faster return to the pickleball court!

REFLECT

This does not have to immediately follow your match. When in bed, I often review in my mind what happened during my match(s). As I recall specific shots or locations on the court that I need to work on, I jot down notes on a small pad I keep in my nightstand. That way, since I know that I have captured my thoughts in writing, I can relax and drift off to sleep. This degree of self-assessment and analysis is something higher-level players do all the time, but, unfortunately, it's something that lower-level players almost never do. Maybe that's why they don't become higher-level players.

"As long as I am prepared, I always expect to win."
— Jack Nicklaus

CHAPTER 4

ORGANIZATIONAL READINESS

There's one more important step in preparing to play your best. You must have all the necessary equipment and related gear quickly available when you step onto the court. Contingency planning will keep you prepared and ease your mind. Think as though you're packing for a vacation. Thoughtful packing will reassure you that you're ready for the unknowns of being away from your home's resources and conveniences. Your pickleball bag is just as important as luggage is to a traveler. You have to be ready for any number of potential issues.

Unlike being on vacation, at pickleball there are no "timeouts" for you to run to the local pharmacy or hardware store. In a recent tournament, I needed to address my chronically sweaty paddle hand in the few minutes I had between games. For some reason, I couldn't locate my rosin powder anywhere in my bag. This pre-match organization error on my part made things doubly worse for me. I became frustrated *and* my grip remained a problem. I was fortunate that my screwup didn't cost me the match. I later found the powder buried in the wrong pocket of my bag!

Here's a checklist of essentials for your bag, plus some advice about paddles, packing, and other equipment:

EXTRA PADDLES

Paddles do break, so having a spare is a smart idea. I recommend carrying your old paddle as a spare if you can't afford to buy two matching paddles when you upgrade. Some players have different types of paddles so they can adjust to opponents, various ball characteristics, weather conditions, or how they're playing on a given day. You might prefer a "power" (harder) paddle or "control" (softer) paddle as your backup, depending on the situation. I like to have a different type of paddle to go to when I'm playing poorly. (Yes, I, too, play poorly sometimes!) Doesn't everyone think they play better after buying a new paddle? That's like thinking that your car drives better after washing and waxing it.

Maybe you have a "lucky" paddle, like Judge Smails had with his lucky putter in *Caddyshack*. Pull out your old "Billy Baroo" or "Selkirk Saber" for that deciding game! Is it the paddle or your mind that makes you feel like you're playing better with it? It might be a little of both, so what could it hurt to switch paddles in the middle of your match? Doing that will most likely give you a psychological boost.

SELECTING A PADDLE

Find a paddle with the largest sweet spot and the roughest textured surface that meets USA Pickleball certification standards. The biggest evolution in paddle technology to date involves surface texture. The more "grit" the better because this allows for increased spin and control. The paddle surface *does* make a significant difference. Dozens of companies produce pickleball paddles: Gamma, CRBN, Paddletek, Franklin, Prolite, Vulcan, Engage, Gearbox, and Selkirk are American companies that manufacture high-quality paddles.

As a Selkirk ambassador and advocate, I'm admittedly biased toward their products. Selkirk was the sport's first company to develop a separate research and development branch: Selkirk Labs. I like being able to play with the latest technological advancements. It helps my shot making and gives me a psychological edge over opponents. I never want to feel that I lost a close match because someone had better equipment than I did. Keep in mind that you can't spend your way to playing better. *A 3.0 player who buys a new $300 paddle is still a 3.0 player!*

PADDLE WEIGHT AND SHAPE

A lightweight paddle enables superior maneuverability, regardless of your size or strength. You may have heard of advanced players adding lead tape to their paddles. A heavier paddle generally means that your shots will display more power. If this is what you seek, then try adding a 12" lead-tape strip around the top edge of your paddle. If your paddle is twisting in your hand while making shots, and stability is what you want, then put the lead tape on both sides of the paddle, down near the handle.

Paddle shape is a matter of preference. The more-natural shape for former tennis players is a slightly elongated paddle. Two-handed-backhand players tend to prefer paddles with extended handles (5+ inches), such as the Selkirk Vanguard 2.0 Mach 6. One of the latest changes in paddles is the new "open throat" design. "Open" means that there's a smile-shaped opening at the bottom of the paddle face, just above the handle. Manufacturers claim that these openings make their paddles less wind resistant, allowing for a quicker swing through the hitting zone, thus generating more power. This makes theoretical sense, but I can feel no noticeable difference in the few that I've tried. Since I use a two-handed backhand, these openings make my hand placement more difficult. You may be intrigued with open-throat models, but be sure to try one out before opening your wallet, and, of course, don't just buy one simply because it's "smiling" at you!

Edgeless paddles are also starting to become common. "Edgeless" means that the paddle doesn't have a black, heavy-plastic protective edge around its perimeter. I like this idea because it provides a slightly larger hitting surface and adds a little more maneuverability. I recommend adding a thin layer of some kind of protective tape to the top half (to midway way down both sides) of an edgeless paddle, to serve as an edge guard. You'll eventually scrape that paddle on the court surface.

Paddle manufacturers are in fierce competition with one other and they're constantly pioneering various innovations to win your business. They tout every "improvement" as a must-have. In 2024, over 500 new paddles are expected to will be submitted for official certification. Try to think critically and see through the marketing hype. You probably won't play better with a paddle just because *tennis strings* are embedded into its hitting surface.

Many players believe that using the latest, greatest paddle will give them an edge. A paddle may make a *slight* difference in your quality of play, but it's your *belief* that the paddle will make you better that's more effective. If you *think* a newer, more "technologically advanced" paddle can make you play better and more confidently, then keep buying paddles. Using that logic, it's reasonable to assume that buying enough paddles will someday put you on the pro circuit! The truth is that the amount of money you spend on a paddle does not necessarily make it better than a less-expensive paddle. My paddle of choice for many years was the mid-priced, Selkirk Vanguard 2.0 Invikta. This still is a fine paddle but recent innovations have made me fall for the Power Air by Selkirk. I have found the increased amount of surface grit is helpful for putting more spin on my shots and thus, providing me more control. Remember ball control is far more important that power in pickleball.

Pro players and manufacturers both say that a paddle that's used 3-5 times per week is good only for about a year. After a year, you may begin to experience dead spots, specific places on the paddle's face where the ball doesn't respond the way it does on the rest of the paddle. When this happens, it's a good time to donate the paddle to a school or other sites where the game is being introduced. Note that the texture on the surface of your paddle can also wear out rather quickly. Selkirk claims that their texture lasts longer than that of other paddles on the market but that period is only a few months, according to their research.

PADDLE GRIP SIZE AND TYPE

When selecting a paddle, you'll often have a choice among standard, thin, or larger "double" grip. I find none of these grips ideal. When I complained to my practice partner about tendonitis in my forearm, she immediately knew what was wrong and how to fix it. This accomplished, advanced player is not only a retired certified hand therapist but also author of the book *Why Do Our Hands Hurt?* She showed me that gripping power comes from the fourth and fifth digits, the ring and pinkie fingers. According to her, 50 percent of hand strength comes from the pinkie helping the other fingers. When the index and middle fingers are the primary "grippers," tendonitis may occur.

In order to allow these two smaller fingers to grip the paddle more firmly and enable the index and middle fingers to execute a softer touch, the grip needs to assume a conical shape, tapering from larger to smaller, top down. To accomplish this, remove the handle's butt cap, which makes the bottom area of the handle as narrow as possible. Then build up the handle's top portion with an overgrip or two. Your pinkie and ring fingers can now more strongly grip the paddle and you'll be less susceptible to tendonitis. I recommend buying the standard grip option and then customizing the paddle as noted. I have never had "tennis elbow" or other arm pain since making this change. As Kenny Loggins sings, *I'm Alright, nobody worry 'bout me.*

SHOES

Far too many players don't put much thought into their shoes. Other than your paddle, there's no more important piece of equipment than your shoes. Ideally, you should pack an extra pair. I have seen players stroll onto a pickleball court wearing boots, "dress" sneakers, running shoes, and even some weird things that had elevated heels! Pickleball requires a lot of quick lateral (side-to-side) movement, pushing off and stopping, so much so that it's possible to tear out the sides of your shoes, separating the upper from the sole. If that happens at a tournament and you have no backup shoes, you'll have to either forfeit or play barefoot! I once saw a tennis player try to play barefoot; it wasn't pretty, even on a clay court. The simple solution: pack a spare pair.

There must be at least a million shoe manufacturers out there, so it's hard to say whose shoes are best. When choosing, the key factors are comfort, strong lateral support, and a quality sole. I recommend replacing the cheap "sockliner" with a quality full-length insole, one that provides firm arch support. You should have different shoes for indoor and outdoor play. A soft-rubber sole is best for indoor play. I play with shoes made for volleyball. They have a soft, tan-colored, gum sole and are designed for extreme lateral movement.

Outdoor play requires a hard-rubber sole. Generally, the harder the rubber, the more expensive the shoes will be, but they will last longer on hard courts. Use your pickleball shoes for pickleball only! Don't wear them around the house, for walking, exercise workouts, or casual wear. I suggest waiting to put on your pickleball shoes until you're at courtside. Don't be the person who stops play because you tracked in water, ice melt, or some other substance onto the court with your pickleball shoes.

Any type of court shoe is fine for pickleball. You don't need a shoe that is marketed specifically for pickleball. Just as with certain types of paddles, "high-tech" pickleball shoes won't kick your game up to the next level, as sometimes claimed by a few shoe marketers. A court shoe is designed for lateral movement as well as forward movement. Running and walking shoes are designed only for forward movement and are a bad choice for pickleball, and they can increase the possibility of rolling an ankle, causing one of the most painful and disabling injuries an athlete can suffer. Basketball, volleyball, racquetball, and tennis shoes are all fine for pickleball. Be sure to check the soles regularly for tread wear. Playing with worn-smooth soles is like driving your car with bald tires — dangerous!

CLOTHES

Obviously, you'll want cool, comfortable sharp-looking clothes that up your confidence factor. In other words, dress for success. If you look like a top player, you — *and your opponent* — might believe it! I have to admit, though, that I've seen a lot of pickleball players who *look* like a million bucks but play like $1.98.

Always pack a spare set of clothes, especially on hot days. Wearing fresh clothes going into the second half of a hot August tournament could actually give you a psychological edge and work against your opponents who might now see you as a fresh, revitalized player, while their sweat-drenched shorts are causing little puddles to appear on the court.

SAFETY GLASSES WITH TRANSITION LENSES

I HIGHLY RECOMMEND WEARING SAFETY GLASSES FOR TWO REASONS:

1. If you ever see a player get hit in the eye with a ball, you'll never second-guess wearing them again.

2. Wearing eye protection provides extra confidence to stay anchored in the ready position at the kitchen line, even when the ball is being hit hard at you. Transition lenses will automatically help with sun glare, and you won't have to fiddle with separate sunglasses. Wearing regular glasses may be more dangerous than wearing none because of the possibility of shattered glass entering the eye.

You may be wondering why the pros don't wear eye protection. Well, they *should*, but they don't because their opponents are so talented that they rarely misdirect or foul off a shot, plus, a pro's self-defense reflexes are incredible. Ben Johns, currently ranked world #1 in singles and men's and mixed doubles, is known for having the fastest reaction time in the game. He can easily handle any ball hit towards him at any speed. Ben is a superior athlete and only 23 years old. You're probably not a super athlete and your twenties might have been decades ago.

Everyone knows reflexes decline with age, but did you know a recent study found the brain's response time begins to decline at age 24! Time makes us all more vulnerable to injury; it will even slow down Ben Johns someday. Note that most eye injuries in pickleball actually come from tipped balls fouled off from the end of partners' paddles, "friendly fire," you might say. I know most players are not wearing eye protection and you are likely one of them. I could give you numerous gruesome eye meets a rock hard pickleball stories but I don't want to give you a flashback to those driver's education crash videos we all had to endure. If you want to play pickleball for rest of your life, please wear eye protection.

MONOGRAM YOUR BAG

This will prevent someone who owns a similar bag from accidentally carrying away your bag. It will also add a bit of a "Wow" factor to your aura. Opponents might get the impression that you're really good because you carry such a cool bag. In fact, they might even think that you're sponsored by the bag company! I knew a female college tennis player who was intimidated by an opponent's huge, monogramed bag. Her coach had to get her a bigger bag to help her regain her confidence.

OTHER ESSENTIAL ITEMS FOR YOUR BAG INCLUDE:

- Sunblock lotion (sweat-resistant)
- Sunscreen lip balm
- Hats
- Extra grips
- Towel
- Sweat bands (wrist and head)
- Rosin bag/tac rag
- Jump rope (for warmup)
- Food (Power Bars, bananas, various carbs)
- Water bottle (carry extra containers on hot days)
- Prescription medication(s)
- Ibuprofen or Tylenol
- First-aid kit with tape for cuts or blisters
- Spring clamp for car keys (Imagine trying to play while thinking your keys are lost!)

Believe it or not, all this gear fits easily into my Selkirk Tour Backpack. There's even a pouch for an extra pair of shoes, sometimes referred to as "the doghouse." Many companies now make similarly sized bags. Think how easy it is to be prepared, yet players often are not. Sweat rolling into your eyes can be a reason why you don't play your best. Hunger can be a distraction. Think of all the potential pitfalls to peak performance that you've eliminated just by having a fully stocked, well-organized bag!

You may have noticed that "cell phone" was not on my list of essentials for your bag. Cell phones have become part of many people's anatomies, but it's a pint-sized distractor. I call cell phones the single, most-damaging thing to happen to the educational process during my teaching career. Even if a person is not actively using his or her phone, part of them is always listening for a notification of some kind to come in. Studies have shown a significant drop in grades for students who carry cell phones during instruction. It stands to reason, then, that the same is true on the pickleball court.

Phone noises are prohibited in tournaments and are simply rude to other players during recreational play. I have heard some players say, "I'm a businessman and my calls are important!" but I have never seen one stop in the middle of a point to answer their phone. So, I ask, "Why can't you put your phone on silent and check it between games?" If you're expecting a call of vital importance, then explain the situation to your fellow players. Otherwise, turn off the ringer, put it away, or better yet, leave it in your car and eliminate yet another distraction!

> "Organization begins with awareness of what
> doesn't work for us."
> — Author unknown

CHAPTER 5

THE FOCUS FACTOR

Golf and tennis must be the two most difficult sports to play. All sports demand that players be focused but these two require so much concentration that audiences are expected to be completely silent when players hit the ball. Silence is so important that it is strictly enforced by officials. When necessary, a tennis umpire will say, "Quiet, please!" to as many as 20,000 people in the stadium. The U.S. Open tennis tournament in New York even arranges to have planes re-routed to avoid player distraction. In golf, officials stand in front of the crowd holding up "Quiet" signs prior to any ball being struck. No other sport makes demands like this. These two acknowledge the tremendous focus required to execute shots.

I'll bet that basketball free-throw shooters and baseball batters would relish the quiet rule in their respective sports. I once had to shoot a free throw with cheerleaders yelling, "See that basket, see that ball, come on screwball, hit the wall!" Imagine the level of focus needed to make the game-tying free throw with a thousand screaming fans waving their hands directly behind the basket, or to hit a 97-mph fastball. It takes incredible focus to play any sport well.

Webster defines *focus* as "a center of activity, attraction or attention, a point of concentration." Others say that focus means "selective attention," to the exclusion of everything else. In Chapter 2, I emphasized exceptional focus as central to achieving peak performance. There is considerable evidence to prove that the best athletes in any sport have an amazing capacity to call upon laser-like focus whenever needed. Somehow, they have acquired the necessary skills to block out various distractors, personal problems, and situational pressure. The ability to focus is not innate; it is a skill that can be invoked and sharpened. This chapter will explain how an average person can improve his or her ability to focus and use that pointed concentration to play better pickleball.

EXAMPLES OF IMPROVED FOCUS

In 1941, Hall of Fame baseball player, Ted Williams, was the last man to end a season with a batting average over .400. When asked how he accomplished this feat, he explained that he was blessed with superb eyesight and a special ability to focus. Flight surgeons tested his eyesight as he trained to become a WWII fighter pilot and found his vision to be that of one in 100,000, better than 20/10, uncorrected. Williams said that he could read the label of a spinning record, just as he could read the spin of a baseball the second a pitcher released it. He would adjust his swing accordingly and could actually see his bat contact the ball. Extraordinary eyesight was a great asset for Ted, but without his intense ability to focus on the ball, he wouldn't be among the best hitters of all time.

When I was a junior high school teacher, I learned about the strong connection between *desire* and focus. Many of my students had been clinically diagnosed with Attention Deficit Disorder (ADD), making it difficult for them to concentrate for extended periods and they required special teaching accommodations. I found it interesting that many of those students were devoted hunters. They would proudly show me pictures of their conquests which told me that they could sit silently in a tree stand for hours while waiting for passing prey. It also meant that they had the focused skill to effectively use a rifle. Thus, concentration can be honed if motivation is strong enough. When it comes to pickleball, how strong is *your* motivation these days?

I experienced how to improve my focus when I was a graduate assistant in college. My job was to drive a legally blind professor to his classes at various branch campuses in Southern Indiana. He liked to listen to audio books during the long drives and had his own cassette player that featured a variable-speed control. The problem for me was that the professor liked to play the tapes fast, which made the narrator sound like Mickey Mouse. I couldn't understand a word and it distracted me while I drove. I voiced my complaint, so the professor agreed to temporarily return the tape speed to normal.

The following week, he asked if he could start advancing the speed again and I reluctantly agreed. Amazingly, after a month of driving, I was able to enjoy his novels at Mickey Mouse speed! Now, many years later, I still enjoy audio books on long drives but am frustrated that my car stereo doesn't speak Mickey Mouse. I'm in debt to my professor for showing me how to improve my concentration. Unfortunately, he didn't show me how to improve my driving!

This is how I began to understand that I was good at focusing my concentration on a single task but terrible at multitasking. Studies have shown that people risk accidents when they multitask while driving. There are good reasons for laws against drivers using cell phones while on the road. You don't want to be a passenger in my car if I'm talking on the phone. I once drove *20 miles* past my planned exit because I was engrossed in a phone call. Unfortunately for me, this was a time when employers valued multitaskers. My pickleball friends know that I lose track of the score frequently. I rarely play with anyone who's worse at that than I am! The reason, I think, is because I'm so completely focused on the various mental aspects of playing well. How common is it that no one can remember the score or who served last after a long, intense point? This is because the point required great focus.

Experts are now finding that multitasking decreases overall work quality. Employers now want *singularly* focused minds. Thus, do your best to be laser-focused when playing pickleball.

FACTORS AFFECTING FOCUS

Let's understand what can cause you to lose focus. How can a professional football wide receiver drop a perfectly thrown ball when no defender is near him? NFL receivers are elite athletes with masterly ball-catching skills, yet you can see them drop balls almost every game for one simple reason: They allow their focus to switch from catching the ball to what they want to do next. It's a simple matter of *not staying in the present moment.*

Focus is all about staying in the present, *the here and now.* In pickleball, you must focus on the shot at hand and not the shot you missed a minute ago or the consequence of missing the shot you're about to make. I'm sure that most of you can relate to points where you battled hard, making multiple highly difficult shots on your way to the kitchen line, only to dump your opponent's easy pop-up into the net. This is like getting all cleaned up, putting on your best clothes, buying flowers, and *not* getting a date! The problem comes from a split-second relaxation of focus due to what your mind perceives as a much easier shot, a shot not worthy of maximum concentration.

EXTERNAL DISTRACTORS

Outdoor tournaments take on a carnival-like atmosphere, with vendors hawking their products, enticing smells drifting from food trucks, loud laughter coming from players' tents, and frequent loudspeaker announcements. It can be a mental-focus nightmare. With any outdoor play, weather can be a major distractor that gets a lot of attention. Bright sun, excessive heat, and, especially, wind can all become enemies of your focus. Playing indoors doesn't make focusing much easier, either. Many of you play on multipurpose courts, with numerous differently colored lines crisscrossing the court's tennis and/or basketball lines, while balls from adjacent courts roll onto your court.

My most exasperating experience with these distractions happened when the court on which I was playing was marked with red kitchen lines, green sidelines, and blue baselines, the three primary colors. To make matters even worse, if that was, in fact, possible, there were at least two other colored lines next to them! It was an absolute mess to play on and making line calls was laughable. Add to that the number of times that the neighboring court of beginner players hit balls onto our court and to say my focus skills were put to the test would be putting it lightly.

Indoor tournaments come with a minefield of distractors, too. The Gamma Pickleball Classic in Pittsburgh holds its matches on the shiny, slippery cement floors of the David Lawrence Convention Center. Imagine the noise of 40-some pickleball matches being played while hundreds cheer and mill around while booming loudspeaker announcements ricochet off the walls. This all takes place in a huge open space under a domelike roof that reflects and amplifies the noise down onto the players. Under these circumstances, focused concentration can take a quick holiday. Distractors like this can challenge the mental toughness of even the most experienced veteran players. Players that do well in this tournament have superior focusing skills. For tournament conditions like this, it's critical to arrive early and give your mind and senses time to adapt.

Your opponents are external factors that can disrupt your focus, too. Doubles players who communicate loudly with each other, speak while a point is being played, or grunt with their strokes can be quite distracting, but those behaviors aren't against the rules. Tactics like stacking (where both players line up on one side of the court during the serve or return of serve) or switching (when players switch sides after the serve) can also distract. There are good tactical reasons for teams to use either of these tactics but one chief reason is to keep you thinking about *them* instead of concentrating on your game.

When you see these tactics, do your best to ignore them. Think, "If I hit a good third-shot drop, it won't matter what they do." Sometimes opponents might say or do things intentionally to upset your focus (see Chapter 12 on gamesmanship and trash talk). While you should try to ignore blatant attempts to break your concentration, you can choose to retaliate, in kind, if that's your style. I take ploys like this as a challenge and use them to my advantage since they pour gasoline on the fire of my motivation, focus, and competitiveness.

INTERNAL DISTRACTORS

The body and mind harbor a seemingly endless sea of distractors. Maslow's hierarchy of needs theory is useful to understand why this is. Maslow lists physiological needs as being most essential. So, if you have not satisfied your body's physiological need for food, water, rest, and waste elimination, you're going to be seriously distracted from playing pickleball. If you have not met your physiological need for clothing, then your *opponents* are going to be seriously distracted and most likely horrified!

The remaining basic human needs that Maslow lists: safety (job security), love and belonging (friendship), and self-esteem and self-actualization are common issues that could be turning over in your mind when you walk on the pickleball court. It's hard to focus on a game when your boss has just threatened your job or when you're having marital problems. You even may not *want* to play, but most everyone is dealing with some kind of issue, so we play on. You must be able to manage *life stress* before taking on *court stress*. Failure to do so will divide and dilute your focus and you *will* play poorly. Hopefully, pickleball takes your mind off of life's stressors, at least for a little while.

TRAIN YOUR BRAIN

By now, you should see the importance of focus. It may well be the most important factor in how you play on a given day. So, how can you become more focused? The short answer is: *You must train your brain.* A supremely focused athlete can intimidate and put fear into his or her opponent. An unwavering and fully focused player who is distracted by nothing can cast a chilling effect. For me, the athlete that personified *pure* focus is tennis great, Bjorn Borg. Borg was a Swedish player known for his steely calm demeanor. He never showed enthusiasm after hitting a great shot or disappointment when missing an easy one. He was always cool under the greatest pressures. The only emotion he ever showed was at the moment he won Wimbledon when he fell to his knees in celebration. Borg's demeanor served him well. His quiet, stoic manner helped him handle the highs and lows of elite match play and his incredible ability to focus made him one of the all-time greats. You may never be ranked #1 in pro pickleball, but learning to focus like Borg when you're on a pickleball court is *not* impossible.

I've used games and techniques to help improve my ability to concentrate. As I share some of these with you, keep in mind that it all starts with your mind being rested. Sleep deprivation is a significant negative in sports, resulting in difficulty remembering, slower reflexes, and a decreased ability to focus. The same effects result from dehydration. Experts say that hydration enhances cognitive functioning. Assuming that you're already getting the proper amount of sleep and fluid intake and have a well-rested mind, let's take a look at some brain-game techniques that can increase your CQ: Concentration Quotient.

GAMES FOR YOUR BRAIN

Here are some fun ways to improve your ability to focus:

Heavy thinking games like chess, Sudoku, Jigsaw, and crossword puzzles all require memory-improving concentration. Remember "Simon" from the late 1970s? This battery-powered game created a series of tones and flashing colored lights and required players to repeat the displayed sequence, with each advancing display arriving faster. I remember enjoying the game as a teenager. It's a great exercise for focus training and you can still buy it today at many retail outlets.

My grandmother and I played a game called "Concentration." We played by spreading out a face-down deck of cards on a table in neat rows and took turns turning over two cards at a time and then turning them face down after noting what they were. The object is to remember the location of the revealed cards and then pick up matched pairs. When all the cards are off the table, the player with the most cards wins.

Two of the simplest focused-concentration games you can play are trying not to blink for three minutes and trying *not* to bite a lollipop. Remember the commercial: "How many licks does it take to reach the center of a Tootsie Pop?" Even the wise old owl couldn't resist very long.

A pickleball-specific game to improve focus is to do a volley-volley drill at the kitchen line with a tiny rubber ball the size of a golf ball. This challenge will force your mind to concentrate and your reflexes to react fast. After just a few minutes of volleying (no bounces allowed!) this tiny ball, you'll know why this drill is so effective. When you switch back to a pickleball, the ball will seem as big as a *softball*. Some of these games may sound juvenile or even like a waste of time, but trust me, they all work!

Focus techniques. Now, here are some more serious methods for training your brain. They're not difficult but they do require some practice. The more you use these techniques, the more comfortable you will become with them and your confidence in their effectiveness will increase. When your mind "credits" one of these techniques for success, it will become part of your regular game-prep plan.

Deep breathing is the single most powerful technique to help improve focus. For years, mental health professionals have been recommending various deep-breathing techniques to help relieve stress, anxiety, and depression. Sleep experts recommend it as a method to facilitate relaxation. Athletes in most sports use deep breathing to speed recovery when winded.

When cameras show a close-up of a professional basketball player preparing to shoot a free throw, you'll typically see an excellent example of deep breathing. This is done not only to help them catch their breath but also to help them refocus. Yoga uses controlled breathing to help control the body and quiet the mind. Pickleball players can use breathing techniques for all of the above reasons and as a way to gain the strong personal advantage of regaining focus. Some of these techniques sound like medical procedures and others have catchy names, but the following steps are all you need to remember:

1. Completely fill your lungs with a deep breath through your nose.
2. Hold your breath for a second or two.
3. Exhale through your teeth to ensure that you exhale *slowly*.
4. Repeat, as needed, or as time permits to regain focus.

Inhale the good and exhale the bad. Use this approach when you feel the stress of a big point or when frustration mounts after missing a few shots.

I usually do this on the way to picking up the ball or prior to serving. This is also an excellent practice during a timeout. Professional basketball players have only ten seconds to shoot a free throw, but still have time for one deep-breath ritual. Pickleball players have the same ten seconds to hit a serve so there's plenty of time to do this during play.

Speaking of a good use of a time out, I was watching the exciting conclusion to a second round March Madness basketball game featuring Marquette University versus Michigan State, when a timeout was called with three minutes to go. The sideline reporter shocked the commentators by announcing that Marquette University Head Coach, Shaka Smart, was *not* giving any instructions to his team. He actually called time out to lead the entire team in a deep breathing exercise! Further investigation revealed that Marquette employs a full-time mental skills coach and the entire basketball team does an exercise almost exactly like the one I describe in the next paragraph before each game.

When you have more time available to do deep breathing, such as in between matches, look for a quiet place to lie down, then close your eyes and relax. I have used my car for a quiet place. I'll change shirts, crank up the air conditioning, as needed, recline the seat, and place my hand on my stomach to feel the rise and fall of my mid-section as I breathe deeply. Focusing on that rhythmic, calming movement serves as a welcome distraction from the stresses of the present. After 10 minutes or so of this, I find that I've calmed myself enough to reset my focus. Before leaving my car, I like to turn up the stereo to recharge my adrenaline and prepare to do battle once again!

Emotional Freedom Technique (EFT), commonly referred to as "Tapping," is another great focusing tool. This approach combines principles of ancient Chinese acupuncture with modern psychology. When tapping was recommended to me, I just rolled my eyes (maybe you're rolling yours, too), but if you've never tried it, you should because it works and costs nothing. There is scientific evidence that tapping lowers levels of the stress hormone, cortisol. It also reduces symptoms of depression and anxiety.

Relax; *no* needles are involved, just your fingers! You've no doubt already experienced some form of tapping, like nervously tapping your fingers on a table or when you test a melon for ripeness. That's all the more force that's needed. The taps send calming signals to the brain. You can tap on any part of your body that hurts, but the goal is to help the brain to focus. So, where should you do your tapping? On your head! Here's the sequence:

1. Eyebrows

2. Beside and below each eye

3. Under the nose

4. On your chin

5. Finish on top of your head

6. Repeat eight times

Psychologists recommend quietly repeating a comforting phrase to calm you while you tap. Say something like, "I'm feeling stressed, but I choose to relax now," at each tap point. Tap at a calm pace. You can also invoke a positive affirmation, such as, "I'm feeling more relaxed now, I love pickleball," or "I love pickleball, but I love Dave Satka's book *more*!" Tapping is an effective way to distract your mind from stress and reset your focus.

A Deep Tissue Massage Gun came to me as a loaner during a recent tournament to help me relieve pain in my lower back. After only a few seconds using this magic machine, my back felt great! I completely forgot the anxiety I felt from playing in my first mixed-doubles tournament. This became another refocusing tool for me. My partner and I went on to win the tournament! The DTMG was the best recommendation I had received in years. Try it; you'll like it.

Meditation seeks to integrate mind and body. There are several types of meditation, including yoga. All types of meditation essentially train the brain to relax through breathing, which refocuses its attention away from stressors and onto something more positive. It's used for many emotional and physical well-being issues. Harvard neurologist, Dr. Sara Lazar, has published findings stating that people who meditate have thicker prefrontal cortexes compared to people who do not meditate. The prefrontal cortex is the region of the brain behind the forehead. This region is considered the brain's "Control panel." It is the part of the brain that helps you control emotions and concentration (focus). These studies also concluded that older participants had the most benefits from meditating. The National Center for Biotechnology Information (NCBI) and several other studies support Dr. Lazar's findings. There is no doubt meditating is a very healthy thing to do and it is a great way for pickleball players to improve their ability to focus on the game.

Quick-fix tips help when time is short. Cold water facial immersion — dipping your forehead, eyes, and cheeks into ice-cold water — stimulates the vagus nerve, which connects the brain to abdominal organs and controls various bodily functions, including digestion and heart rate. Decreasing your heart rate will allow your mind to calm down. Once calm has been restored, you will have a chance to reset your focus. Lastly, caffeine *really* works! Coffee, energy drinks, and dark chocolate all stimulate the brain and can help with focus. Use them in moderation, of course.

TIPS FOR FOCUSING ON THE COURT

"Look" the ball into the paddle. If you played Little League baseball or softball, your coach probably repeatedly told you to, "*Look* the ball into your glove." This was sound advice because it forced players to stay in the present moment. Errors happen when players think about "what's next?" — anticipating where to throw the ball before actually catching it. Pickleball players need to be like Ted Williams. Try to watch the ball hit the paddle. This level of focus will help you hit the paddle's sweet spot more often and keep you from looking up to see where the ball is going. Stay in the present. Do one thing at a time, do it well, and *then* move on.

Watch the spin of the ball. Being able to quickly recognize the type of spin on a pickleball is critical. Just as Ted Williams was able to recognize a curveball, slider, or fastball from its spin, a pickleball player must be able to recognize topspin, underspin (slice), and sidespin on a pickleball. This will allow you to know in advance where the ball is going, how it will bounce, and how to put your "bat" on the ball, just like Ted. You don't need to have Ted's eyesight, just his *focus*.

Use good footwork as your foundation for excellent shot production. I detail the fundamentals of good footwork in Chapter 8. Footwork should be one of your primary areas of focus for the "mechanical" (as opposed to mental) aspects of pickleball. When your focus is distracted and your game is off, footwork can serve as your "go-to" remedy. Concentrating on developing quick feet, bouncing, and moving to get your body in perfect position to hit each shot can serve as the "reset button" for your focus. You also might get to enjoy the psychological reward that comes from suddenly playing well again. Let your feet tell your brain where your focus should be.

FOCUS WINS!

If you play pickleball long enough, you'll eventually find yourself on both the positive and negative ends of big comebacks. Have you ever wondered how a team can lose when ahead 10-2? Conversely, how can a team that's down by eight points in a game to eleven go on to win? The answer to both questions is *focus*. There is a tendency for a team with a big lead to relax and play some loose points. Danger, and a critical loss of focus, visits a team that thinks the game is over before the final point is played. Their mind has moved from the present moment to the next round, or to getting a drink, or maybe to posing with a smile on the medal stand. This is a recipe for disaster.

If this happens in combination with the currently losing team rallying the resolve to forget their lost points of the past and focus on the opportunities of the *present*, then a comeback turnaround could happen. Playing one point at a time can turn the tide. Often, a large score disparity is due to many unforced errors. A couple of serve returns into the net, two or three attempts at low-percentage shots, and a dumped dink here or there can turn a game into a blowout loss fast. Getting back to basics, using high-percentage shots, gives a losing team a chance.

When I'm in a situation like this, I'll often say to my partner, "Let's make *them* win this next point." Give your opponents a chance to gift your team with some free points. Once a comeback is mounted, pressure will begin to rise on the team that once had the big lead. If they handle this pressure poorly, a comeback can gather real steam. Remember that you're never totally out of it in pickleball. That's one of the great qualities of the game. Yogi Berra said it best, "It ain't over 'til it's over."

> **"At the end of the day, you can't control the results; you can only control your effort level and your focus."**
> — **Ben Zobrist, 2016 World Series MVP**

CHAPTER 6

THE BRAIN GAME

In Chapter 1, I discussed how my development of the mental side of tennis transformed me from a mostly losing college player to a winner. After years of being concerned only with my own play, I finally realized that I had to be just as focused on my opponents. I started paying much more attention to my opponents' strengths, weaknesses, and tendencies. You could say that I became an investigative reporter, researching all available information about whom I'd be playing. My notes included their reactions to weather and responses to my tactics on court. Their body language even gave me some key insights. My goal was to gather as much data as possible that could help me win. As my tennis IQ increased, so did my wins. The purpose of this chapter is to help you discover the game *inside* the game of pickleball, the elements that will increase your *pickleball* IQ and give you the winner's edge.

Pickleball is one of few sports where older, wiser players can beat younger, more athletic players. The team with the younger, faster, stronger players usually wins in professional sports. That was the case, until 43-year-old Tom Brady won a Super Bowl by outthinking the other guys. At almost twice the age of most players in the NFL, Brady was easily the *least* mobile quarterback in the league, but his football IQ was far superior to any other quarterback in the league. It's always great to win by outplaying your opponents, but when you win by *out-thinking* them, it's particularly rewarding.

HOW TO IMPROVE YOUR PICKLEBALL IQ

Every new opponent is a puzzle for you to solve. You need to make a game plan based on all the information you can gather about him or her. One way to do this is to "scout" them. Try to arrive early at the courts and watch your opponents' warm up. Don't be obvious by pulling up a chair to take notes, like a baseball scout does. Just watch them (if you're playing doubles) practice while you casually chat or stretch nearby. The first thing to check is the dominant hand of each player. Lefties can be troublesome because of their shots' natural spin. Watch them hitting as many types of shots as possible: ground strokes, volleys, overheads, dinks, serves, etc. Do you see any obvious weaknesses or favored shots? If you're lucky, you might overhear a complaint about a sore knee or shoulder, the weather, or some other distraction. You never know what type of "intel" might be useful when your battle begins.

If you're seeing an opposing team for the first time, collect as much information as possible during the pregame warmup. Evaluating opponents is considerably more difficult in pickleball than it is in tennis because in doubles, you'll be warming up across the net from your own partner instead of one of your opponents. However, you can still collect some basic information from being on the same court. Again, watch for lefties. During the first game, hit a wide variety of shots at them early on to get the answers to these questions:

- Does a particular kind of shot cause one or both players difficulty?
- Are their third-shot drops effective or do they miss them frequently? Do they even *use* third-shot drops?
- Do they recoil fearfully when you hit hard shots at them?
- Are they slow when moving forward or do they fail to use a "split step" (see Chapter 8)?
- Is there a particular type of spin that either player has trouble handling?
- How are their respective ready positions? Do they lower their paddle after the first shot (see Chapter 8)?

Take advantage of players who stand straight-up and are slow to react to balls out of their reach, or if they lower their paddle after hitting the first return. Take note if a player tends to hit certain shots to the same place on the court. For example, some players like to drive forehands down the line or hit overhead smashes in the same direction most of the time. See if both opponents enjoy dinking or try to avoid it. How's their body language? For example, an exasperated shoulder shrug after netting a backhand drive could indicate that the player is struggling with that shot. Early in the game, determine if one of your two opponents is significantly weaker than the other. If so, you and your partner should target that player on big points.

Bottom line — and this is important — it's time to stop being the gracious loser! Use all this carefully gathered intelligence to systematically dismantle your opponents and become a gracious *winner*!

If I would have done a better job of evaluating my opponents in a recent tournament, my results might have been much different. My partner and I lost the first game and were being soundly beaten in the second, when, out of desperation, I tossed up a lob from the baseline. It wasn't a very good lob, but our seemingly flawless opponents dumped it into the bottom of the net. My partner asked me, "What are you doing?" emphasizing the point that lobbing from the baseline is usually a poor choice.

My ploy worked, though, so I tossed up another lob, which, like my first one, ended up being blasted into the bottom of the net. Amazingly, they booted a third lob, too, but on the fourth one, the stronger player called off his struggling partner and smashed it away. They held on for the win, but we nearly pulled off a smart comeback due to discovering their weakness. Had I done a better job scouting or testing them during play, we might have won.

PREGAME DECISIONS

Using your brain to outsmart your opponents can allow you to gain the upper hand before the first ball of Game One is struck. Be aware of your environment and constantly evaluate your game. The beauty of all these pregame strategies is that none requires you to be a great player, or even currently playing well, to gain an advantage. Before your match, do you ever give any thought to which side of the net you prefer to start, or if you want to serve first or receive? A smart team will have already decided the side from which they want to start serving and whether they want to serve first or second. There's plenty to consider regarding both decisions. Experienced teams will make a thoughtful, strategic choice based on careful observations.

SIDE-SELECTION CONSIDERATIONS

If the sun or wind is a factor, take the more favorable side for the first game in a best-of-three match. This way, you'll have the advantage if the match goes to a third, deciding game. In a single-game match, you might want to choose the less-favorable side to start, in order to have the sun or wind at your back the second half of the game, after the change of sides. Coaches from all sports always say, "You can't win the game in the first half" or, "A good half doesn't make for a victory." Typically, the team that wins the *second* half, in any sport, usually wins the game. On the other hand, being in the lead at the halfway point tends to make opponents change strategies and puts pressure on them to up their game. Sometimes merely making a firm declaration about side or serve will cause opponents to wonder about your resolve. Once, after one of our opponents slipped in a shaded area, where the sun had not yet dried up the early morning moisture, I heard him say, "That's why they wanted the other side so much."

Even in indoor tournaments, your choice of sides can lead to a major advantage. One of my recent events was held in a large multi-sport complex. The pickleball courts were taped off in a huge open area on a hard-rubber floor. The background was a solid-white wall on one end and clear netting on the other. The netting was in place to prevent balls from rolling onto a large artificial-turf field used primarily for soccer. The netting offered no contrasting backdrop and made it very difficult to see balls coming from that direction. Our opponents won the right to choose first and, out of reflex, chose to serve. I chose the side that faced the white wall and they even agreed not to switch sides at midpoint, since we were playing indoors with no sun or wind issues. By the third round of play, I noticed that *all* the teams were aware of the backdrop issues and demanded that sides be switched at the halfway point. We enjoyed a significant advantage for two full rounds all because of my pregame observations. I'm so smart, I should be in the Mensa Pickleball Society, right?

THE SERVE-OR-RETURN DECISION

Many players wonder if there is an advantage to serving first. The debate is between scoring first or having two serves on your first serving opportunity. Mathematically, there's no advantage. Giving only one serve to the starting team perfectly balances what would otherwise be an advantage to the first server. Statistically, even though the receiving team always has an advantage, it does not mean that they are more likely to win the game. Some say that there's a psychological advantage to being in control first. A powerful serve can further enhance this advantage. Rarely do players play their best during the first game. Even professionals experience some tightness or nervousness before hitting their stride.

Therefore, it may be a wise decision to let the other team serve first since they will be forced to make the more difficult third shot. If you're feeling nervous or had a poor warmup, it may be wise to return serve first, so that you'll have an easier third and fifth shot. My final thought on the first-serve decision is that jumping out to a lead, possibly a big lead, can impact the rest of the game and that's always a possibility. Playing from ahead is a big advantage. Many very confident players always want to serve first for this reason. There's really no wrong decision here. Just make your decision using your best rationale for the moment at hand.

IN-GAME EVALUATION

Many games are lost by teams that fail to self-evaluate and make adjustments after the game's first half or after losing the first game in a best-of-three format. Einstein defined insanity as "Doing the same thing over and over and expecting different results." Obviously, then, many pickleball players practice insanity, continuing the same tactics after being soundly beaten a few minutes earlier. You must do *something* different to change your fate. If you're struggling to make a third-shot drop, then start driving your returns. If your opponents are eating up everything you hit hard at them, slow it down and vary your shots, mixing hard with soft.

Sometimes your tactics may be sound, but your execution is faulty, or your opponents are just playing extremely well. Be honest and admit that you're playing poorly and use one of the refocusing tools from Chapter 5 to get your plan back on track. If your opponents are on fire, be patient and try to weather the storm. Conversely, if you're winning, don't change tactics. *Never change a winning combination!* The old country adage applies here: "Dance with the one who brung ya," which means stick with the strategy that puts you in the lead.

Pay close attention to your opponents and you could gain some key insights during the game. Maybe they're getting tired or suffering ill effects from the sun. Maybe they're tense or nervous. In Chapter 1, I mentioned defeating the #1 seed in my college tennis conference tournament, but I didn't mention that I hit a 20-mph bloop serve on match point! That was clearly the biggest point I had ever played and I hit a serve that I hadn't hit the entire match. I had been banging hard serves all match long, but this time I put myself in my opponent's shoes, thinking that if I were him, I'd be looking for the Big One down the middle or The Kicker out wide. He was nervous and paced the baseline, so my match-point strategy was to float a "cupcake" to his big forehand and hope that he would over hit it. I hit my floater and he did his part by blasting it into the bottom of the net! Incidentally, my coach hated that serve but loved getting the win.

OUTTHINKING "BANGERS"

A banger is a player who hits almost every ball hard. They'll dink only when they can't bang. Your strategy should be to force a banger to deal with your dinks and returns that land in the kitchen (non-volley zone). Just as with tennis racquets, technological advances in pickleball paddles are enabling harder hitting. Pickleball's popularity is attracting stronger, better athletes who have more ball-striking ability. I've found that former tennis, baseball, and racquetball players are more inclined to favor a hard-hitting game and this has led to an influx of bangers who love to be in control, ripping balls for clean winners and striking fear in their opponents' hearts. In my opinion, this is *not* strategic pickleball!

It takes little pickleball IQ to play this way. However, if this tactic didn't work, it wouldn't be so popular. I know that there are lots of players who get frustrated playing bangers. I linked up with a 4.5 level group in Florida that actually bans bangers from joining! Maybe you feel helpless because you're not powerful enough or lack the lighting-fast hand speed to counter these ultra-aggressive players. But...*have no fear, Big Dave is here!* There are ways to *outthink* — and *defeat* — this one-dimensional, Neanderthal, style of play.

Remember, pickleball is a game of making fewer errors than your opponent. Hitting the ball hard all the time is high risk. Your job is to make them pay for playing so aggressively. First, I'll answer the question: Why does banging work? Then, we'll get to how to counter the person(s) who are terrorizing your local group. I believe this strategy works at the 4.0 level and below because when balls are coming hard at someone's body, their natural instinct is to defend themselves. Bangers are *counting on* you reacting this way. Their plan is to hit you with the ball or force a weak, defensive return. They don't consider where their shot would land if no one touched it.

The quickest way to get a banger to stop whacking balls at your chest is to *get out of the way!* Any ball hit unusually hard that clears the net by a foot or more is going out. Usually *way* out. In Chapter 9, I discuss in detail how to stop hitting out-balls. I also tell of how I just walk off the court whenever one of our club's classic bangers takes a big backswing on his strong forehand. I know that his shot is coming hard, right at me! Once a banger realizes how smart you are and that you're *not* going to play *their* game, you'll force Banger Boy to adjust. This is my favorite anti-banger strategy. But wait; there's more!

If you intend to stay at the kitchen line and defend yourself from a banger, here are some winning tips. First, *get ready*. Remember this phrase, "The harder they hit, the lower you get." Bend those knees and establish a great ready position. Get your paddle up, throat high, and have the tip of your paddle pointed at 10 o'clock (90 percent defensive position) or 9 o'clock (100 percent full defensive). Do *not* attempt to swing or punch the ball back. This will only hit the ball back to the banger and allow him or her to take another big swing at you. Just block the ball with your paddle tilted slightly downward and soften your grip. The idea is to block your return short or at your opponents' feet if they are near the kitchen.

In Chapter 4, I recommend wearing eye protection, for both safety and added confidence. Leaning forward at the kitchen line, face first, is when you need that confidence. Eye protection can also limit your fear of injury when facing off with a banger. A seasoned banger is like a dog. They can sense fear. If you recoil, turn sideways, squeal, or display the slightest bit of intimidation, the banger-dog will continue to bite you. You need to be James Bond cool, with a martini in one hand and your Walther PPK paddle in the other. You can easily block back blast after blast if you're in a strong defensive position. Don't worry; it won't take long before your local banger will blast one into the net or you'll sidestep one and listen to it smack off the fence. You'll be the talk of the club after they see how coolly you handle the brutal bangers and send them packing!

Another solid tip is to try to keep all your shots low. This means using slice instead of topspin anytime you have to drive a shot. The backspin will make the ball skid, keeping it low, forcing your opponent to hit up. Most returns hit hard with an upward trajectory usually go out. Only highly skilled players (4.5+) have the consistent ability to put extreme topspin on a ball, get it over the net, and have it land inside the baseline.

My last tip for playing against bangers can be summarized in three words: soft, softer, and softest. This means that dinks, resets, and deep, high-floating returns of serve are your best friends. Power loves power. *Never* try to speed up a shot or drive one past a banger. Force bangers to generate their *own* power on shots. Soft shots are kryptonite to a banger. They have no patience for dinking and they hate doing it. Make them have to think and actually strategize a point. Let them take all the risk, too. Focus on keeping the ball in play with high-percentage cross-court shots (see Chapter 9) and let them bang their way into oblivion.

PICKLEBALL IQ TEST

The best pickleball IQ test I know is the "Stanford-Binet-Satka Test." Okay, I'm sure that Stanford University and old Alfred Binet want no part of me. My test is better, anyway, because it's much simpler and pickleball specific. All you have to do is think about a team or friend you play against regularly.

READY? HERE COME THE HALF-DOZEN STANFORD-BINET-SATKA TEST QUESTIONS:

1. Can you give a full "scouting" report on him or her right now?
2. Can you write down all of their strengths, weaknesses, and tendencies? (I know a player who actually keeps notecards on opponents in his pickleball bag.)
3. Do you know which strategies or shots work well against them?
4. Do you pick up on little bits of information these opponents display that can give you an edge? (A casual comment like, "wow, that sun is tough today," should be your cue to throw up a few extra lobs.)
5. Does their body language ever indicate circumstances you can exploit?
6. Can you name at least two tactics to frustrate them if one is a banger?

If you can readily answer these questions, then your pickleball IQ is pretty high. If you find that you progressively have more success against these opponents the more times you face them, then your IQ is approaching brilliant. If your "scouting" report helps you regularly *beat* them, plus occasionally beat players significantly better than you are, then you're definitely genius class and have earned a lifetime MPS membership (Mensa Pickleball Society)!

> "I think most of success is really mental,
> because I ran against a lot of individuals who
> were probably more physically talented,
> but I was able to outsmart them and
> outthink them and out-prepare them."
> — Edwin Moses, two-time Olympic Gold Medalist

CHAPTER 7

MENTAL TOUGHNESS

E xperienced players will tell you that winning at pickleball is a far greater *mental* than physical challenge. The number of mental variables is vast, and they are much more difficult to manage and control than physical aspects, such as fitness and shot production, which can be easily measured.

Athletes know exactly what they need to do to fine-tune their games and peak physically. Pickleball players younger than 45 usually say that the game is about 75 percent mental and 25 percent physical. Even the best players tinker with their shot mechanics and work to maintain peak fitness for about a quarter of their time. Those illusive mental variables are of far greater concern to top players. Players' personal-life circumstances can have a significant negative impact on their performance when difficulties arise off the court, testifying to the importance of that 75 percent mental factor. Strangely, most instructional videos, Internet articles, clinics, camps, and in-person lessons concentrate almost entirely on that 25 percent physical side of the game.

For decades, professional sports teams have poured their resources into the physical matters. Strength and conditioning coaches, physical therapists, and athletic trainers have long been considered essential to building a winning team. Only in the past few years, though, have *mental-skills* coaches been added to team staffs. Mark Cuban, owner of the Dallas Mavericks, for over two decades, has been on the forefront of mental health training for his players. In 2015, the Cleveland Browns hired the first Director of High Performance. This position supervises all elements of athlete preparation, including mental health. Today, most major sports teams employ or contract sports psychologists.

It's also important to note how aging can alter the mental-to-physical ratio. Players with decades of experience know how to prepare and have mastered the mental side of the game. Life's challenges still happen to senior players, obviously, but they are usually issues that have happened before and get handled without major consequences to their game. Many seniors feel that their physical health and well-being present the greatest challenge to their success on the court. A top-ranked senior professional player once told me that, for her, the game is only 25 percent mental and 75 percent physical. She confided that her physical condition became a primary concern after turning 55, and if she now arrives at a tournament feeling well, she's confident that she'll win. At this point in her career, she has few, if any, concerns about her game preparation.

I am sure you agree that being mentally tough is a great quality to have in pickleball and in life. The question is, how can I be more mentally tough? The good news is that mental toughness is a skill that can be developed. It is a form of emotional intelligence. Being mentally tough is not genetic but it is something wise parents begin to foster at a young age. People of all ages become tougher mentally by overcoming adversity. Although it is extremely difficult to watch your child fail, watching them dust themselves off and try again begins to develop toughness. Mental toughness is a survival skill that all mammals in the wild attempt to pass down to their young. The philosopher that coined the phrase, "What doesn't kill you will only make you stronger," understood strength through adversity.

Mental toughness defies stereotypes. For example, you may know a mild-mannered, soft-spoken woman who is tough as nails and able to maintain focus and purpose regardless of the situation. Physical stature and sheer muscle strength are inconsequential. History provides many examples of those who have shown incredible resiliency in times of crisis. Gandhi was a small-statured, somewhat frail, professional man who became the epitome of mental toughness. How tough would a person have to be to endure savage beatings, not defend himself, and survive month-long fasts, in order to achieve freedom and equality for others? Another example, this one fictional, comes from one of my all-time favorite movies, *Cast Away*, starring Tom Hanks as Chuck Noland. **Spoiler alert!** As a passenger on a plane that crashes into the ocean, Noland is marooned on a deserted island with only a handful of tools, but he manages to survive there for *four years* before being rescued. Noland is a superb example of someone who *learns* how to be mentally tough. Billy Joel, in his song *Pressure*, sings, "Here you are, in the ninth, two men out and three men on, nowhere to look but *inside*, where we all respond to pressure." Joel knows that mental toughness lies deep inside all of us.

Mental toughness is the crown jewel of all sports elements. It separates the very good from the great. World-renowned trainer Tim Grover says, "Mental toughness doesn't guarantee you'll win, but playing without it pretty much guarantees you won't." Being mentally tough means that you have the ability to stay positive in the face of overwhelmingly adverse circumstances. Great athletes will tell you there is nothing more motivating than failure. Mentally tough athletes find solutions, not excuses, when faced with adversity.

THERE ARE THREE PERSONAL CHARACTERISTICS THAT ALL PICKLEBALL PLAYERS CAN BOLSTER TO IMPROVE MENTAL TOUGHNESS:

1. **Self-confidence.** Drawing on prior experience to be able to say to yourself, "I've done this before" and a belief that you can do it again. All pickleball players will find themselves in what appears to be an impossible deficit in a game. This is the time to recall that incredible comeback you invariably have made in the past. Be optimistic. Anything can happen in pickleball.

2. **Determination.** You must be willing to "dig deep," bear down and say, "I am not going away." In times of adversity, turn up your focus and your hustle. Make your opponents earn every point. Be tenacious.

3. **Patience.** There are numerous on court factors that can test the patience of a monk. You can learn to shrug off distractions and adapt to any circumstance. Comebacks are slowly made, one point at a time. There is no 3-point line in pickleball.

Some say that you can develop mental toughness the same way you develop muscles, by using your brain to repeatedly "lift" the weight of adversity upward toward positivity, the more "reps," the tougher you become. The remainder of this chapter details five common pickleball challenges (weights) and explains how to overcome (lift) them. Your improved self-confidence, determination and patience will fortify you as you tackle these challenges.

HEAVY "LIFTING" IN PICKLEBALL

I love the Navy SEAL motto: *Deal with it.* External environmental factors like wind, heat, sun, and noise affect players on both sides of the net. Who will "deal with it" better? Experienced players adjust to conditions *before* walking onto the court. They'll also adjust to conditions as they change and adapt a strategy to exploit challenges such as poor play, bad line calls, blowing a big lead, or other unsettling happenings.

Here's how to lift some of those heavy challenges:

#1: OVERCOMING WEATHER CHALLENGES

WIND: FRIEND *AND* FOE

Pickleballs are essentially Wiffle Balls. Trying to hit them, even in a mild, unpredictable wind is frustrating, but everyone who plays outdoors will eventually face a brutal breeze. Watching a pickleball being blown around on a windy day can be funny but is usually maddening. Many players complain about it, refuse to play in it, or blame it for their losses. Mentally tough players, though, *embrace* the wind and calculate how to use it to win. Third-shot drops and lobs are actually *easier* to make when hit against the wind.

A strong head wind will knock the ball straight down into the kitchen. Powerful drives are also easier to keep in the court as the wind pushes back against the ball. Crosswinds can make it easier to attack a player's weaker side. This is a good time to use sidespin on the ball and let the wind amplify the curve of its trajectory. When the wind is at your back, play more conservatively. Let the wind carry your shots deep, to keep your opponents back. Players who emit an "I love playing in the wind!" vibe have a huge mental advantage over those who complain about the conditions.

BEATING HEAT AND HUMIDITY

My motto is: Love a hot summer day and rise above those who don't! One time, my partner and I went into the deciding game of a tournament medal match being played on a sultry summer day. I was really feeling the heat and decided to take a knee in the shade between games. My partner whispered to me, "You know that *every* ball is coming to you now." He saw that the opposing team took note of my distress. At the moment, I didn't really care, but after the final game started, I quickly realized that he was right. The old saying, "Never let 'em see you sweat!" had suddenly become a reality for me. I was suffering and the balls were all coming my way. I had to dig deep and summon all my experiences when I had to deal with intense heat fatigue on the tennis court.

That win was especially memorable because it was due largely to mental toughness more than simply outplaying our opponents. In hindsight, it would have been wise to have my partner take a knee with me, to take the spotlight off of me. If you can will yourself to overcome heat, you can mentally crush an opponent. At the half-game court switch on a miserably hot day, demonstrate how unfazed and fresh you are by jogging to the other side of the net and bounce on the balls of your feet when ready to return serve, even if it's the very last thing you feel you can do. This is the kind of mind-over-matter mental toughness that's bound to deflate your opposition.

THE BRIGHT-SUN CHALLENGE

Even top pickleball pros' mental toughness can break down. Leigh Waters had a famous meltdown because she was being targeted for lobs hit into an intense sun. She incorrectly believed that, in general, it was poor sportsmanship to take advantage of the sun, and she screamed in protest at her opponents. Of course, this did nothing but get more lobs sent her way. Her outburst nearly cost her team a gold medal (and cash), but her then 15-year-old superstar daughter/partner, Anna Leigh, stepped up to control her anger and rescued the deciding game.

Waters' big mistake was letting her opponents know which of her buttons to push. In a situation like this, never let your opponents know, either by your complaints or negative body language, that the sun is bothering you. If you do, you'll open the door to lobs galore, lurking in the sun. Letting a sun-drenched lob bounce in order to make a safe return is no sin. You can also take a timeout to confer with your partner to see if she/he can handle any sun lobs better.

#2: FLIPPING A BAD DAY

Thoughts of disappointing your partner, frustration, or even anger, commonly come over players having a bad day. It's tough to stop this train of negativity as it speeds down your tracks, but confidence in your mental toughness can derail it. *Think* your way back to positivity! Slow things down. When opponents are on a roll or sense that you're in the mental dumps, they tend to speed things up. Counter this by getting a drink, wiping your paddle grip, or toweling off. Take some slow, deep breaths, as I describe in my chapter on Focus.

The hardest thing to do is to stop thinking about all your unforced errors or the suddenly bad mechanics of your shots. Start to focus on your footwork. Hit your most reliable shots. Play to the middle of the court. Don't try to blast your way out of your funk by trying to force winners. If more drastic measures are needed, try playing "George Costanza" pickleball. Do the complete *opposite* of what you had been doing, which got you into this mess in the first place. George was a habitual liar that started telling the unfiltered truth. If you're a dinker by nature, then start banging! If you're a banger, then start dinking.

#3: CONTROLLING EMOTIONS

ABC's *Wide World of Sports* melodramatically summarized the emotional extremes that come from athletic competition as "The thrill of victory...

and the agony of defeat." During an athletic competition, there will be emotional peaks and valleys. Successful athletes must learn how to keep their highs in perspective and their lows under control during play. Since pickleball is a game of "runs," it lends itself to frequent ups and downs. It takes determined mental toughness to remain calm and battle your way out of a pickleball valley.

I believe that a major source of players' negative emotions comes from the very thing responsible for pickleball's massive growth — the game is *so* easy to learn. Because it is so simple to play, failure can be extremely frustrating. Your brain may scream, "How could you miss that dink?! It's just a Wiffle Ball, floating slowly over a little net, *and you can't tap it back?!*"

How you deal with the frustrations of playing poorly and losing is the key to being a mentally tough player. Some players look like nothing bothers them. Others will curse their poor play, acting out angry body language or even screaming. A few will erupt physically, slamming their paddle, whacking the ball into the backstop, or hitting something nearby. Tennis legend John McEnroe is one of the most famous examples of this type of behavior. Rising pro pickleball star Darrian (DJ) Young became the first player to be fined for spiking his paddle after losing the match point. His paddle bounced off the ground and ricocheted into fans seated court-side. If you feel the need to vent your frustrations, I recommend doing it in a private place. Step outside for some air if you are playing inside or go to your car for a few minutes, if playing outside. Before returning to the courts, tell yourself you are starting fresh. Your aggravating play is now a thing of the past.

There's a fine line between self-loathing and self-correcting. Some players denounce themselves as a way of regaining focus. Others chide themselves to *stay* focused. Some tell their brains to reactivate the muscle memory stored inside. Mild self-correction that refocuses resolve and determination is perfectly acceptable. Harsh personal degrading, though, is counterproductive and cringeworthy. Chastising yourself tends to tighten muscles and nullifies relaxed playing. Another reason for restraint is to avoid giving any useful intel to your opponents. A comment like, "I haven't made a decent dink all day!" will invite a dink storm from savvy opponents.

Show yourself some compassion to quiet your inner critic. A gifted golfer once gave me some great advice during a round when I was loudly degrading myself for yet another slice into the woods. He said, "Dave, you aren't good enough yet to be getting so mad at your play." His words hit home. Did I think I was on the PGA tour? I was just a casual golfer who rarely practiced, *not* Tiger Woods. Pros have the right to be upset after missing a well-grooved shot they've made thousands of times. Give yourself a break. No one is perfect and everyone makes mistakes. Stay positive with your attitude and encouraging words: "You're better than this! I'll play better next game!" or "Hang in there! I've overcome slow starts before," or "If I concentrate on my footwork, my play will improve."

Don't misunderstand, though. Showing emotion on court is not all bad. Don't appear to be in a stoic trance. A fist pump with an emphatic "come on!" after a great point can supercharge your team to victory. Self-peptalks are an important part of the power of positivity. The emotional highs I get from playing well are addictive. I'm always looking for the type of competition that can bring me my next high. That's why I play this game. One example of my peak on-court fun is the rush I get from hitting the game-winning shot "around the pole" (ATP). An enthusiastic burst of emotion after hitting a great shot is *not* being disrespectful to your opponents. Celebrating an opponent's error *is* considered poor sportsmanship unless it's match point. Feel free to show your enthusiasm on the pickleball court. It's part of the game.

One final note: Being down, disappointed, or even depressed doesn't mean that you're not mentally tough. *It's how you respond* to these emotions that determines your degree of mental toughness.

> **"As hard as the moment is that you are in, the more you have to remind yourself, the more you have to talk to yourself."**
> —**Novak Djokovic, 24-time Grand Slam Tennis Champion**

#4: BREAKING OUT OF A SLUMP

Breaking out of a serious slump is one of the most difficult challenges an athlete can face. A slump is an *extended* period of poor play. Most athletes go through a slump at some point. Slumps can be psychological or a result of flawed mechanics, but should not be confused with the neurological condition Focal Dystonia, a.k.a. "The Yips," suffered by professional golfers and baseball players. This is a rare condition affecting fine motor skills due to the overuse of muscles. When Yips happen to famous athletes, it's headline news.

Star baseball players like Steve Sax, Steve Blass, and Chuck Knoblauch were all at the top of their profession, then, tragically, dropped to the bottom in an instant. In 1997, Knoblauch was an All-Star and Gold Glove Award-winning second baseman. After the season, he was traded to the New York Yankees. As a Yankee, he started to make an increasing number of throwing errors. In one game, he made three throwing errors in six innings. He asked to be removed from the game and never again regained his accuracy throwing to first base. The Yankees were forced to make him an outfielder and eventually traded him away.

David Duval was the #1-ranked golfer in the world. He then had some minor injuries and serious relationship troubles that forced him to take a break from the tour. Upon his return, his top-notch game had left him. He could not make the cut at a tournament for two seasons and was no longer invited to play. He eventually did regain his skills, but not until joining the senior tour, 20 years later. *That's* The Yips.

What I'm referring to in pickleball is a plain old slump. It usually starts with a particularly bad day or two on the court that causes a significant loss of confidence. That loss of confidence, combined with a weak support system or poor coping mechanisms, causes play to spiral down into Slump City. It's very difficult to stay positive when you're playing far beneath your usual standard.

Probably the best advice I can offer for slumpers is to step away from the game for a while. Go on vacation and leave your paddle at home. Don't watch pickleball on television or YouTube. Maybe even avoid your pickleball friends if they always talk about the game. Try to clear your mind of everything related to pickleball. Wipe your hard drive clean, so to speak. I believe that many slumps are brought on by the pickleball "rut." Playing the same way, against the same players, day after day, can create a malaise and a decrease of focus. Emerging flaws in shot mechanics can also increase the onset and deepen the effects of slumps, so stay alert for those warning signs.

A player I know had a most unusual service motion. He served with his hand on *top* of the grip instead of behind it. The motion was so unusual that it grabbed the attention of experienced players. It was a fundamentally flawed technique but this player used it successfully for several years, even winning a tournament at the 4.0 level. Then one day, he started missing numerous serves. The next time he played, he missed even more. His serve got so bad that the receiver's partner had to stand off the court to avoid being hit by what's known as "a Nasty Nelson."

This man refused to change this deeply-engrained fundamental flaw. He tried a long break from the game, then practiced his flawed serve hundreds of times, but he never was able to serve more than a couple balls in the correct court again. He completely lost confidence in his ability to serve and was forced to quit the game he loved. Was it the Yips or just a severe slump? Maybe it was a combination of both.

Busting a slump comes down to your degree of mental toughness. You must be strong enough to admit that you need to take a break from the game. Then you need to have the will to self-evaluate your game and commit to fixing what's wrong. Ask a knowledgeable friend to help, or pay for a lesson to rebuild the troubling shot(s). Before returning to the court, spend some time visualizing yourself playing at your best. *Don't play again until your confidence has been restored.* Go to the court relaxed, avoid thinking about the past, focus on your footwork, and have fun. Before you know it, your slump will be over and your new winning streak started!

#5: PERFORMING UNDER PRESSURE

Many professionals, such as airline pilots, surgeons, and emergency dispatchers, to name a few, must perform under pressure as part of their work. Performing artists and pro athletes have to perform under pressure *and* do it in front of an audience. Everybody loves a dramatic ending to a big game, but what's it like for the players on the court or field when thousands of cheering fans expect a game-winning performance from them? It takes a ton of confidence, nerves of steel, and maximum mental toughness.

There may be no greater mental high than performing well in front of an enthusiastic crowd. Having played basketball in Indiana, I competed in packed gymnasiums with screaming crowds, venues as raucous as any elsewhere in the country. I vividly recall those electric environments. One of my fondest memories comes from blocking a shot against the backboard and hearing the roar of several thousand fans. Fun fact: Indiana has 14 of the 16 largest high school gyms in America, with an average seating capacity of 7,500.

Performing poorly in front of an audience can be psychologically devastating. The lives of some high-profile athletes have been permanently marred because of their shortfalls on the biggest stages. (You might want to look up the World Series saga of Boston Red Sox first baseman Bill Buckner.) It's easy to find pickleball players who play well when nothing is on the line, but put these same players in front of a crowd, with a tournament medal at stake, and some will melt down facing that pressure. When there is "nowhere to look but inside," you'll find the true measure of yourself as a player. The great ones play their best under intense pressure. You may not be on the PPA or MLP tour yet, but when the chips are down, even in a local club event, dig deep and stick with your natural, normal game. Sometimes heroics can emerge from solid, everyday fundamentals.

TIPS FOR PLAYING RELAXED UNDER PRESSURE

The recent rise of professional pickleball tours has put the country's best players in stressful situations. Most current pros had minimal experience playing in front of large crowds. Now, on tour, they must perform in front of many thousands, on television, and at huge pickleball venues. Plus, they must earn a living competing for prize money. Maybe you're not a pickleball pro, but you *can* prepare your mind to deal with the anxiety and nervousness that comes with being under competitive pressure.

There's no single solution. You have to develop your own *personalized* coping mechanisms. Just because you aren't playing on TV for thousands of dollars doesn't eliminate the pressures you feel when playing at your local club. You might experience the pressures of playing in a tournament, or maybe when you're the last game to finish in your recreational group, and all your pickleball friends gather to watch. The key is your belief in yourself and your confidence in your game.

The success of any coping mechanisms you employ starts with a sound playing mindset. Ideally, you need to go into a stressful situation with a "relaxed alertness." Think like a Jedi and "Let the force flow within you," or assume an attitude of controlled aggression. Anxiety and adrenaline combine to produce pressure. Too much of either ingredient can hinder performance. On the other hand, a moderate balance of both anxiety and adrenaline results in a great recipe for obtaining peak performance.

Here are a few tips to help you keep anxiety and adrenaline in balance at moderate levels:

DEVELOP RITUALS

Tennis great, Rafael Nadal, is famous for his on-court rituals that help him maintain focus and relax under pressure. Before every serve, he repeatedly bounces the ball, touches his nose, ears, and hair, and tugs at his shorts. Novak Djokovic, Nadal's main rival, bounces the ball repeatedly, like Nadal, before each serve. Incidentally, these two superstars' extended pre-serve rituals were a main reason for the implementation of the serve clock, which limits pre-serve preparations to 25 seconds. This has helped to shorten match length.

Lea Jansen is currently the #2-ranked women's singles pickleball player. She uses her paddle to touch both shoulders, hips, and ankles in a figure 8 pattern before every serve. Lea stated on the Tyson McGuffin podcast that a sports psychologist recommended this ritual as a way to "reset" her emotions. I personally like to bounce the ball a couple of times then once between my legs before a serve. You can develop your own special ritual. Be creative; just make sure to do the same thing every time. If you happen to lean toward an OCD lifestyle, you probably already have on-court rituals, even though you may not be aware of them.

BREATHE

As I emphasized in the previous chapter, deep breathing is one of best things you can do, both on and off the court. It's an excellent way to regain focus and deal with stress. You breathe in "the good" and slowly exhale "the bad" (stress) of rising pressure. Controlled deep breathing can feel like a weight being lifted off your chest.

STAY IN THE MOMENT

Focus only on what you can control. Try putting a treasured memento or meaningful symbol of some type in your bag that can take your mind off the situation. Some players put a favorite joke in their bag. One pro has an app on her Apple watch that sends her motivational quotes. Remember, it's just pickleball. Play like you have nothing to lose. It takes time to build trust in these techniques, so be patient. Beware, though; your cerebral cortex may be "sore" the first time your brain lifts off all the "weight" of pressure.

> "Tension is who you think you should be.
> Relaxation is who you are."
> — Chinese proverb

EFFECTS OF MENTAL TOUGHNESS ON OPPONENTS

Being a mentally tough player is not only an ace in the hole for yourself but also can have a significant effect on your opponents. Nobody wants to face a supremely confident, "I can handle anything!" competitor. Players like this send an intimidating message. *You* can become intimidating once you're in peak condition and confident in your game. So, how does this intimidation factor work?

Start by entering the court bouncing on your feet, eager to go, like a boxer before the bell rings. When play starts, apply maximum effort to your movements, get to the kitchen line hungry, like a wolf seeking prey. Get into a crouching ready position, as you look to engage "the enemy" in an aggressive dinking battle. You don't even have to hit the ball hard to be intimidating. Let your lively movements and expressed spirit *be* your intimidation. Even if you lose the first dinking battle, your demeanor will show your opponents that they might have been lucky that you missed. They may wonder, "Why would this guy/gal act so aggressively at the kitchen line if s/he didn't love dinking and is really good at it?" Instead of being an intimidating dinker, you can win a bang-bang volley "firefight" at the net, hit a big forehand drive, or execute with great gusto whatever your favorite shot may be.

An aggressive first point can sometimes set the tone for the rest of the game. In one tournament I played, I came in with the mindset, "I can out-dink anybody; I'm the best dinker on the court!" The first time both teams made it to the kitchen, I assumed an aggressive stance and looked positively eager to get to the ball. When our opponents tested me, I hit several aggressive cross-court dinks, which pushed my opponent left and right until he dumped one into the net. I pumped my fist and told my partner to be ready. "They won't be dinking my way again anytime soon!" That was intimidation through action.

A friend of mine is an excellent but impatient dinker. Instead of having an "I am going to out-dink you!" attitude, he'll quickly try to change directions, speeding up the ball, or go for an extreme angle. His mindset needs to be, "If you hit four dinks in a row to me, I'll hit eight right back at you. If you think eight dinks will beat me, then I'll hit *sixteen*!" Demonstrating an iron will and a "*Bring it!*" aura imposes your mental toughness on your opponent. If an opponent believes that dinking is a losing proposition, she/he will be forced into hitting lower-percentage shots. By taking away the dink as an option for your opponent, you'll have significantly increased your chances of winning. Sometimes, the highest compliment you can receive comes from opponents who avoid hitting the ball to you.

Thus, to be an intimidating player, you must have a "Never say die!" attitude. This means that you *never* quit during a point. You run to drop shots or angled shots, even if you know you can't reach them. You play even *harder* when your team is losing, particularly when it appears that you have no chance of winning. Never show weakness or that anything bothers you on the court. Opponents *will* pick up an aura about you and they'll respect you for your hustle and tenacity, in victory or defeat.

After acquiring this profile of toughness, when you ask your latest conquests to "Say my name," they'll reply, "Iron Mike?" or "Iron Michelle?" You'll then proudly respond, "You're damn right it is!" Shaving your head and wearing a black pork-pie hat might help too. It sure worked for Walter "Heisenberg" White in *Breaking Bad*!

"Concentration and mental toughness are the margins of victory."
— Bill Russell

"Improvise, adapt and overcome."
— Marine Corps Mantra

CHAPTER 8

POSITIONING & FOOTWORK

This is the first chapter to center on ways you can improve your play while on court. Positioning and footwork are both cerebral parts of the game. It takes agility to be in the right place at the right time, but what we're talking about here is more about understanding some basic concepts. Once you understand proper court positioning, your shots will be easier to make, and it will be easier to defend against your opponent's shots.

To move quickly and efficiently to the correct position on the court, you'll need good footwork. Developing effective footwork takes some coordination, practice, and a good balance between your mental and physical approach. Think of good footwork as learning how to be a good dancer. It's not all that much different from the "Electric Slide" or "Samba," but your dance floor is a pickleball court. You just have to concentrate on getting your feet into the right position. Once you do that, agility will take care of itself.

THE IMPORTANCE OF GREAT FOOTWORK

I have seen tennis greats, Jimmy Connors and Roger Federer, practice and play in person. The first thing I noticed was how relaxed and easy they made the game look. Their shots seemed to flow as if they were painting a work of fine art. I also took note of their footwork, once spending 20 minutes just watching Connors' feet! Both of these guys never stopped moving on the court. They were always bouncing on the balls of their feet when waiting for the shot to return, and took small steps to put themselves in perfect position for the next shot. They were never off balance. It's no wonder both of these legends were known for their great footwork..

Both of these men are rather small and slightly built, compared to many of their opponents when they played. For example, at his peak, Connors was just 5'10" and 150 pounds, yet he had powerful groundstrokes. Granted, their hand-eye coordination was probably off the charts, but their superior footwork allowed them to transfer their full weight into their shots by being in the right position to do so. Most pickleball players take footwork-positioning for granted, but their lack of understanding about it is likely to be at the root of their game's problems.

As a young tennis player, I noticed that when I tried to imitate Connors' footwork, it helped my game. Imitation is a form of *visualization*. Imitating a great player's footwork is a mental exercise that anyone can do. When I decided to concentrate on being "light" on my feet, I became a better player. You may wonder why that helped me so much. Well, the reason is that being in perfect position to execute a shot, in any sport, is essential for success.

When pro basketball players are in a comfortable position on the floor, their shoulders square up to the basket, they're perfectly balanced, and they become deadly accurate shooters. The same is true for NFL quarterbacks. When they're on balance, they can step into the throw and complete a precision pass. Major League pitchers try to keep hitters off balance, but when a batter is able to time his stride toward the ball and be on balance at contact, he is probably going to rip the ball hard. Most professional pickleball players do drills targeted at improving their footwork, without hitting any balls. Tyson McGuffin may be the best example of a pro who drills specifically on footwork to improve movement on court, and it shows!

WHAT IS GOOD POSITIONING?

When I coached basketball, my philosophy on defense was to try to force opponents to shoot three feet farther out from the basket than they were usually comfortable doing. I reasoned that Shaquille O' Neal was the best player in the world when he was four feet or less from the basket. At seven feet, though, he became much more ordinary, and, if he had to constantly play 15 feet out, he wouldn't be in the NBA! It takes great positioning and footwork, even for professionals, to perform at their best.

Good defense in basketball is all about forcing your opponent into poor positions on the floor. If you succeed, their shooting percentage will go down and your chances of winning will go up. The same goes for pickleball. Opponents hitting shots from bad positions will miss a much higher percentage of shots than players hitting from good positions. In both sports, you may see a great shot from a player who is way out of position, falling down or otherwise off balance, but that's because they're superior athletes. Even then, it's a relatively rare *Sports Center* highlight. Great athletes get away with poor footwork more often than we mortals do, but not over the long haul. Over a game or two, the percentages tend to play out in favor of the team using sound fundamentals and who hit their shots from a good position.

Pickleball is no different from any other sport in that regard. Good footwork that puts you in the proper position is essential for success. It's the foundation for any good pickleball shot and remember, it requires no extraordinary talent to move your into proper position. A big difference between a 3.5 player and one who is a 4.0 is positioning. Both players can make good shots, but the 4.0 player will be more consistently in the optimal position to return the ball and will make fewer errors. True 3.5 skill-level players may think that they're just as good as 4.0s because they can hit all the same shots, but it's *footwork and positioning* that separates them.

Few players recognize that their footwork is a problem. Great players would be average players without mastering it. I have a unique method to determine if you're in a good position to hit a pickleball. The key is your arm, *not* your feet. Anytime you can make contact with the ball while your arm is bent, you're probably in an excellent position to hit the ball, and likely have already executed proper footwork to make the shot. Conversely, any shot hit with a *straight* arm means that you're out of position with faulty footwork. Pay particular attention to your arm the next time you play. Make a mental note as to where your arm is when you make an error. I think you'll find that shots hit with an extended, straight arm are much more likely to be hit weakly, popped up, or result in an error. It takes discipline to move your feet instead of just reaching for a ball. If you want to see an example of a player using poor footwork, watch someone who switches hands to hit a shot. You'll never see a pro do this unless they are truly ambidextrous.

Most good shots in pickleball originate in what's known as your personal "box" or hitting zone. This space is roughly 12 inches off either hip or shoulder. Another way to measure your hitting zone is to place your bent elbow on your hip while holding a paddle. This is your optimal effective range. A ball hit to you within this range, with your arm cocked, allows you to make a hard, fast return at your opponent, assuming that the ball is at least net high. At a minimum, you'll be able to handle this shot, making far fewer errors than when you extend your paddle out of the box.

This approach also applies to dinking. Tyson McGuffin recommends a dinking drill where you try not to drop a ball tucked into your paddle arm's armpit. This is a great drill to demonstrate how close you must get to the ball in order to minimize errors. Most players are amazed at how demanding this drill is because it pinpoints the reason why so many players simply reach outside the box for their dinks.

Even pros play better when they hit their shots from inside their box. Just like a baseball player who gets a pitch in his hitting zone that he drives for a hit. Swinging at a pitch outside of that zone usually results in a pop-up or ground out. If you remember phone booths, think of your hitting-zone box as a kind of phone booth. Since the ball is not always going to come into your hitting zone, proper footwork will move your hitting zone to the ball. This is how you make your phone booth a *mobile* phone booth, one kind of mobile phone you should keep on the court!

BEST POSITION ON THE COURT

The three most important locations (positions) in pickleball are kitchen line, kitchen line, and kitchen line! Remember: *The kitchen line is the winning line*. There's no better place to be. The kitchen line (non-volley zone line) is the one place from which you can hit down at your opponents. This is where most points are won, and the team that reaches the kitchen line *first* wins 60-70 percent more points. When you're at the kitchen line and your opponents are back near their baseline, you're in control, and a threat to end the point. Your control of the kitchen line puts pressure on your opponents to hit superior shots to stay in the point. Getting to the kitchen line should be your goal every point.

The saying goes, "A mind is a terrible thing to waste." Likewise, a good drop shot that can get you to the kitchen line is a terrible thing to waste. Players at the kitchen line are in position to pick off below-average third-shot drops, which puts pressure on opponents. Of course, the opposite is also true. If you're in no-man's land, between the kitchen line and baseline, you've made it easy for your opponents. You're no threat to them and you open yourself to a hard-to-handle shot at your feet. The rules make it easier for the team returning serve to get to the kitchen line, giving them an edge for point scoring. Think of the kitchen line as the "high ground," the place you fought hard to take. If you control it, you're in command of the battlefield!

ANGLE POSITIONING

If you manage to move your opponent close to a sideline, your team must do two things. First, your team member on the ball side must take away the shot down the line. Second, and more importantly, your other player must slide over and square his body toward the ball to take away the crosscourt angle that cuts through the middle of the court. This is your opponent's high-percentage shot, the place where the ball will most likely go. I recommend exaggerating your coverage of this shot by having one foot well over the centerline. Your coverage of the side and middle will create an opening for a short-angle return, but that is what you want. This entices your opponent to hit a difficult, low-percentage shot. Now you have brought your friend, Mr. Sideline, into the fight. You should always "pinch the middle" when strategizing your positioning.

GOOD FOOTWORK STARTS WITH THE READY POSITION

Once you're positioned on the kitchen line's "high ground," you must assume a proper ready position. A good ready position is when your feet are set slightly wider than shoulder width, with knees bent, your weight on the balls of your feet, and your paddle cocked upward. In this position, you are ready to react to any shot. Remember, you can block a ball driven at your face a lot easier if your paddle is up. You'll have plenty of time to lower your paddle to get to a drop shot. The next time you watch a Major League baseball game, notice the ready position of infielders as the pitcher begins his delivery. These players will already be in the ready position that I just described, but with a glove up instead of a paddle. This ensures that they will be able to protect themselves from a line drive or be able to make a quick move to either side. In between pitches, they'll stand up and relax.

You need to do exactly the same thing in pickleball for the same reasons. Try to jump or move quickly to either side while standing straight up. It's awkward and unbalanced. You need to be posed like an infielder, especially when you're at the kitchen line. Remember my motto: "The harder they hit the lower you get." Movement left or right is called a "slide" in tennis, basketball, and pickleball. You can execute a slide from the ready position by pushing off with the foot from the opposite direction you want to move. Your other foot will make a short lateral shuffle. The foot you pushed off from will catch up with a hop or two, almost clicking your feet together; then you land in the ready position again. Your feet should never cross. In pickleball, you rarely have to slide more than two hops in either direction.

Although your goal is to get to and occupy the kitchen line's high ground, there are times when it makes sense to blow the bugle and retreat. Old-school pickleball strategy was, "*Never* leave the kitchen line," even if you're about to get blasted. This is nonsense! It's okay to retreat, take up a new position, and survive to fight another day.

FANCY FOOTWORK: THE SPLIT STEP

If you do retreat from the kitchen line, you'll find yourself in a place called "no-man's land," or that area between the kitchen line and the baseline (serving line). As every good general knows, there's a *proper* way to retreat; you never just turn and run. To retreat in pickleball, backpedal quickly until just before your opponent strikes the ball. At that moment, you'll execute a "split step." Split steps are like playing hopscotch: three hops on one leg, a jump, and then landing with feet apart (your split step). Of course, retreating is moving backward, but, just before your opponent hits the ball, do a split step to re-establish your defensive ready position.

The same split step is used to move forward through no-man's land, as well. Once you complete a split step, you immediately need to assume the ready position. The key to a good split step is timing. This may take some practice. You can rehearse this in your living room if you like. The purpose of the split step is to stop moving prior to the ball being hit toward you and to be ready to move your body into your hitting zone. Players who do not use a split step can look silly when a soft angled shot goes by them, untouched. It's much more difficult to hit a ball while moving. It's also nearly impossible to change directions and hit a ball at the same time. This is why you move forward, do a split step, move again, and hit the ball.

You must also be in a good ready position before returning a serve. A careless ready position is the prime reason for serve-return errors among inexperienced players. For example, once, when I played college tennis, our team was a huge underdog against the University of Tulsa. The guy I was playing was major-league cocky, and it seemed like warming up with me was a waste of time for him. I won the toss and elected to serve and noticed that a small crowd had gathered to watch. What I didn't know was that this guy was going to try to humiliate me in front of his home-court fans! I walked to the baseline, bounced the ball a couple of times, looked up, and saw this guy standing straight up, with no sign of being ready. He had his racquet at his side. So, being the good sport that I am, I asked, "Are you ready?" He nonchalantly replied, "Yeah, go ahead," which really confused me. Nobody could be ready to receive a big serve looking that lazy.

That was fine with me, so I hammered a big serve down the middle that hit the "T." Mr. Cool could barely react and watched my ace blow by. Fifteen-love. Moving to the ad court, same story, same dialog. Me: "You ready?" Mr. Cool [bored, with attitude, arms at side] "Yeah, I'm ready." "Are you sure?" Getting no response this time and seeing no evidence of Mr. Cool's ready position, I decided it was time for a lesson. Boom! Ace to the backhand corner! Thirty-love.

As I looked up after bouncing the ball for my third serve, I saw the poster boy for Ready Position Awareness Month. Mr. Cool's knees were bent low, his racquet was cocked, and his furious eyes locked on me. Yeah, I had gotten his attention. As I rushed the net behind my next big serve, I felt the air blast of his return rocketing past me down the line for a clean winner. He broke my serve and crushed me 6-1, 6-2. It wasn't even *that* close! Moral: Always be ready-position ready so you don't give lesser players the upper hand!

Another piece of positioning advice is to be sure to serve primarily from the middle of the service box, midway between the centerline and sideline. This allows for a better third-shot drop or drive because you won't have to move as far to get to the ball than you would if serving from the extreme corners. If your opponent serves from a corner, reposition yourself to cut off the new angle they've created. Imagine that you and the server have a steel rod connecting you together at your belly buttons and the rod pivots at the top of net's center strap. As the server moves right, you move left and vice versa.

SPECIALTY FOOTWORK: THE LOB

Retrieving a good lob is the shot that requires the best footwork and is the most troublesome for beginners and intermediate players. Learning the proper footwork can also prevent injury. A good lob will expose poor footwork like no other shot. Typical players backpedal to cover lobs, scurrying backward while facing the net. This results in a staggering, unbalanced movement as they calculate where to strike the lob's high arc. Moving backward fast is both clumsy and dangerous, and can often end in a fall. I've seen players break their arms and wrists trying to "break" their fall, and break it, they did. One such fracture required a screwed-on metal plate plus weeks of pickleball-less recovery. Concussions are also possible when striking the back of the head on the hard court surface. That's why proper footwork is crucial when covering a lob.

Here's how to do it: assume you're at the kitchen line in the ready position when a lob goes up. Mentally, then physically, you must immediately do the following:

Step 1: Take a large drop-set (deep-knee flex) with your dominant leg, pivot on the balls of your feet (turning sideways), and push backward with your non-dominant leg.

Step 2: Immediately decide if you need to turn and run toward the baseline or if you can reach the lob by moving sideways. If you stay turned sideways, you've estimated that you'll be able to get under the lob by sliding your feet, as previously discussed. You need to contact the ball in this position so that you can turn your body into the shot and generate power. It's like punching the heavy bag at the gym while standing face-to-face with it. Imagine how much more power that punch would have if you turned sideways first. The latter is how you want to hit the lob with an overhead smash.

Step 3: If possible, slide quickly into position under the ball. Wait for the ball with your arm cocked, paddle back, above your shoulder. *Always* try to hit the ball in the air. Anytime you're hitting the ball downward, it's a good thing. This is why an offensive lob should be used sparingly, only as a surprise tactic. Never backpedal to get to a lob.

Step 4: If the lob is excellent and you need to run to reach it, don't run to the spot where the ball will land because your body will be in the way. Worse yet, the ball could land *on you*! Give the ball's landing spot a wide berth and circle around it. As you intersect with the ball's bounce, your body's sideways position will allow you to make the appropriate groundstroke. Your best options from this position are, in order of effectiveness, (1) dropping it back into the kitchen (highest difficulty), (2) a high, defensive return lob, or (3) a drive, low over the net.

BASELINE FOOTWORK

Movement along the baseline during rallies should be done by sliding the feet. Sliding means that your feet are never crossed which will allow you to move left or right immediately. Never turn and run after a ball unless it's the only way you can reach it. The most common error players make from this position is to hit off their back foot. Instead of moving their feet into position with their body behind the ball, they reach for the ball and hit off their back foot. I call hitting off the back foot "a Captain Morgan," in honor of a pose by the iconic mascot of that spiced rum and cola beverage. A friend of mine does this so often that I promoted him to "*Major* Morgan." If he keeps it up, I might make him a Colonel! This is not the kind of battlefield promotion you should be working toward! Just remember that you never want to look like a guy on a rum bottle's label when playing!

Almost anytime that your arm is fully extended to hit a shot, it's probably not going to be a good one. Always step forward with the leg opposite your paddle, *toward* the direction you want the ball to go (left foot, for right handed player, etc.). Stepping toward your target will transfer your weight into the shot. This also applies when hitting a dink but be sure that the ball bounces first.

SERVING FOOTWORK

Footwork for your serve should be the same as that for a baseline drive. Right-handers should place their left foot just behind the baseline (to avoid a foot fault) and their right foot behind the left, shoulder-width apart. This is known as a *closed* position (or stance). An *open* position faces the court with both feet just behind the baseline. Toss or drop the ball into the court and use your normal forehand stroke to serve the ball, observing current serve-swing rules. This will transfer your weight forward into the ball. Another excellent method to transfer your weight is to swing your right leg forward, along with your right arm. Once your right leg plants on the court, it can be used to push you back behind the baseline, putting you in perfect position for your next shot. Novices should use this same footwork, but with a pendulum-like arm motion to serve, similar to a bowling-ball delivery, but using a paddle, instead.

GENERAL MOVEMENT

Long strides may be necessary for you to get to the ball quickly, but short, choppy steps are best once you get close to the ball, in your hitting zone, to make your shot. *All* pickleball shots should be hit in front of your body, not from your side, and definitely not by reaching behind. To keep the ball in front of you, get your body *behind* every shot.

One reason pickleball appeals to so many people is the relative lack of movement required, compared to tennis, for example. At lower skill levels, movement can be so limited that a game amounts to not much more than taking a brisk walk. However, if you resolve to get behind every shot, you'll get a considerable aerobic workout.

PLAYING TIPS FOR PLAYERS WITH MOBILITY LIMITATIONS

You might be thinking that all this advice is great, but what if I have a physical issue that keeps me from getting into the proper position? You may be overweight, lack quickness, have bad knees, had a hip replaced, or advancing years have taken their toll. In Chapter 3, I urged you to get as physically fit as you can be. As NFL Coach Chuck Pagano says, "If you don't have your health, you don't have anything." Lifestyle adjustments to your daily diet and exercise regimen are the key. If you have physical issues, do something about them! See your doctor or a physical therapist for diagnosis and treatment. Certainly, some limitations may be difficult to improve, but, if you're a dedicated pickleballer, even small advances are worth your time and effort.

There's a fine player in my group who has troublesome knees. His lack of mobility seriously limits his performance, but he won't seek medical treatment. His only attempt to address the problem was to buy compression knee "braces." He does no stretching, never drinks water on or off the court, and does the usual five-dink warm-up. He is *not* maximizing his ability. On the other hand, there's a 75-year-old man in my club who lost 60 pounds so that he could become a better pickleball player. *That's* what I'm talking about! You have to admire that kind of motivation. Challenge yourself to optimize your body's well-being.

Now, what if you've dutifully addressed your mobility issues but still don't move well? I'll bet you've never seen an instructional pickleball video featuring a slow, overweight, middle-aged man with a bad knee. These types of videos always seem to feature agile, athletic players who can easily transition from baseline to kitchen line. Although I have no permanent limitations to my mobility, I have used all of the following tips to deal with injury or fatigue. My reality is that I can't increase my speed on court, regardless of how hard I train. Even though these tips won't make you faster, they will help you be in the right position all the time.

You'll quickly find the game much easier to play when you no longer have to hit difficult shots from no-man's land. Prepare to hear comments like, "James must have had his Wheaties for breakfast today!" or "Judy's Red Bull energy drinks are making a big difference!" Just smile in agreement. They probably won't even notice your new tactics.

1. Hit lofted returns of serve or old-fashioned "moon balls." This will not only give you more time to get to the kitchen line but also will keep your opponent back by the baseline. You'll get a ton of free points when your opponent tries to overhit this deceptive shot. Hard-hitting bangers *hate* this shot. Try it, you'll like it!

2. Hit lofted third-shot drops. These are the types of drops that arc relatively high over the net then drop almost straight down. Using this skillful shot will reduce the number of your errors and allow you to advance a step or two closer to the kitchen line. Bangers also hate this shot because it slows things down and takes speed off the ball, which they need to bang it back at you. Frustrate a banger today; you'll be glad that you did!

3. Lob when out of position. I'm talking about a high defensive lob. This will give you plenty of time to get back into position. A lob that's falling straight down is the most difficult to smash. You'll be surprised when you see how many errors this shot produces.

4. Cut off angles. If you lack mobility, you must consistently position yourself at the spot on the court where your opponent's next shot is most likely to go. Always try to get to the non-volley line, if you can, before the ball comes back across the net. Force your opponent to make short-angle shots instead of trying to cover all of your side of the court. Every step you take forward reduces the number of your opponents' options. You might look like you're lumbering awkwardly, but moving forward is *always* better than standing still or retreating. Don't worry about being lobbed. It is another low percentage shot just like the short-angle shot. Talk to your partner in advance for help covering lobs. Remember, the kitchen line is where you are going to do damage.

5. Anticipate! Only extremely talented players can disguise their shots. Sensing where the ball is about to be hit is no big mystery 99 percent of the time. Most everyone steps in the direction they want their shot to go, as they watch the ball strike their paddle. Very few players can look one way and hit to the opposite direction. Therefore, if your movement is less than quick, you may need to take some chances and move to where you think the ball is going to go. Don't make your move too early or you'll either leave a big opening or become a target. Start your move at the moment your opponent begins his or her swing.

6. Use underspin instead of topspin. Hitting an underspin ("slice" or backspin) stroke causes the ball to move through the air more slowly, but this is still a sound tactic because the ball will skid when it lands and keeps it low. A ball hit with topspin cuts through the air, dips down quickly, and gets to your opponent faster than a ball hit with backspin. Accordingly, the harder you hit your shot, the quicker it can come back, catching you flatfooted in the dreaded no-man's land.

Is being "vertically challenged" (short) a limitation in pickleball? I don't think it is. Yes, tall players have a longer reach but that also means that they may have a tendency to fully extend their arm and hit more weak shots. The exception to this would be on an overhead smash. Clearly, it's an advantage to be tall when hitting this shot, but those same tall players have to bend farther down to get to get balls hit at their feet.

I think a 5'10" height has some nice advantages. A shorter person is a harder target to hit and can usually evade a ball heading out of bounds more easily. Shorter players can drive a ball straight across the net, as opposed to a taller player who needs to bend down to make a shot off the notoriously low-bouncing pickleball. Probably the biggest advantage for shorter players, particularly those with well-developed thighs, is their low center of gravity. This is important at the kitchen line for maintaining balance when reaching for attackable drops and dinks while not falling into the kitchen. A taller player tends to bend at the waist, which causes top-heaviness and balance issues. So, tall people often don't have an advantage at the kitchen line. I'm often impressed by how many drops or dinks relatively short players can pick off.

HOW TO EVALUATE YOUR FOOTWORK AND POSITIONING

The best way to evaluate your footwork and positioning is to make a video recording of your play. A GoPro camera, for example, can record an entire three-to-four-hour play session, depending on resolution and SD-card capacity. GoPros currently sell for $300-$500 and are useful for many purposes, in addition to pickleball analysis.

If you do decide to record your play, be sure to keep the first recording you make so that you can use it as a benchmark to show your progress. Simply attach the camera to the fence behind one of the baselines on your court for a good overall view of your play. Just forget about it and play normally. Beware, though; most people seeing themselves play on video for the first time are sometimes more than a little shocked. It's much different than watching YouTube videos of the pros, with their elegant footwork that moves them gracefully across the court, putting them into perfect position to execute smooth, flowing strokes. You're probably not going to look like that, but a journey of a thousand miles begins with the first steps!

Watch your video in the privacy of your own home and see exactly how you move on the court. There's no better way to teach proper positioning than with "game film." Watch a second time, specifically for your footwork. A GoPro won't fix your footwork, but it will reveal what you need to do to improve it, after seeing yourself in action at your present level. This critical self-evaluation is why professional coaches in every sport require that their players watch game film.

CHAPTER 9

SHOT SELECTION

This chapter explains another on-court method in which you can use your brain to improve your game. In fact, I believe this chapter is so effective that it can make you 20 percent better in one day! Understanding good shot selection will take some trial-and-error experience, but if you strictly follow my advice, the process will be much shorter, making you a smarter player sooner. Many players make poor shot choices out of habit. If this is true in your case, then the trial-and error-process could last longer. Knowing *which* shots and *when* to use them is often the difference between winning and losing. In fact, I would say shot selection is the single most important factor for winning at the 3.5 level and above.

There are plenty of books about using various shots as a strategy on the court. I aim to provide simple fundamentals for you to make sound shot selections. A strategy is a specific plan employed in certain situations. My advice can be used in any situation and needs no plan. Think of the following advice like your everyday clothes; a strategy would be selecting attire for a special occasion. Below, I'll explain why I say, "It's better to miss the *right* shot than to successfully make the wrong one."

MY FUNDAMENTALS FOR GOOD SHOT SELECTION

#1: HIT TO YOUR OPPONENT'S FEET

This advice eliminates all the consternation about where particular shots should be hit. This strategy is so simple it is brilliant. Anytime you can put a ball close to your opponent's feet there is little chance she/he can produce a return shot that will put you on the defensive. Even better, a shot to your opponent's feet will most likely produce an error. Think of your opponent's feet as a target. If your opponents are on the baseline, then drive the ball to the baseline. If they are in the transition zone, then hit a shorter drive down at them. If they are at the no volley line, then a drop or dink is the shot. If you can program your brain to "Think feet!" your shot choices will become instinctive. A word of caution, thinking feet does not mean looking at them. You still must concentrate on making clean contact with the ball. Looking up early to see where your shot is going is a common mistake that must be avoided.

I know some of you are thinking, "I thought the object of this game was to hit the ball out of the reach of the opponent?" Common sense tells us to hit the ball away from your opponent and into an open area. In doubles pickleball, you must avoid this temptation. For example, hitting a ball short when an opponent is trapped near the baseline is actually doing them a favor. Now your opponent has a ticket to the no volley line or "winning line" as I like to call it. You may think you hit a fine shot but really all you have done is bring your opponent exactly where they want and need to be. If you have been hitting this shot and receiving "Thank You" notes from your opponents, now you know why.

#2: HIT CROSS-COURT

I find it curious that most players hit their pre-game warm-up shots straight down the line, but when the game begins, most shots should be hit cross-court. The reason is simple; the net is two inches lower at the center and you have several more feet of court to land a ball hit diagonally. This also includes dinking.

#3: HIT INTO THE NON-VOLLEY ZONE

This means hitting more shots softly. Any shot hit into the non-volley zone (a.k.a. the "Kitchen") is a neutral shot intended to take away any advantage an opponent might have and bring the point back to "level." It doesn't matter who your opponents are or what they're doing if you hit an excellent, delicate drop or dink into the kitchen. You could be playing

Lindsey and Riley Newman. They could be switching, poaching, or doing all sorts of aggressive moves, but if you hit a good drop shot it doesn't matter. A shot hit into the kitchen is *never* a poor choice. You can refer to a good dink as "the great neutralizer." Only attempt a third-shot *drive* when the return of serve is short and bounces relatively high. Remember: *the harder you hit, the harder it can come back.* As they say in professional golf, "You drive for show and putt for dough." In professional pickleball, "You drive (hit hard) for show and drop/dink for dough."

#4: HIT TO THE MIDDLE OF THE COURT

This will decrease sideline errors and can frequently cause your opponents confusion. After seeing the result of this approach, you'll understand the wisdom of "Down the middle solves the riddle."

#5: GOOD DINKING IS GOOD THINKING

Have you ever wondered why advanced-player games take longer to play? It's because most points include a dinking "Battle." Dinking is the ping-pong aspect to the game and patience is the key. The strategy in a dinking battle is to gradually increase the difficulty of your opponent's next dink. This can be done by hitting a wide dink then a middle dink to make your opponent move or by mixing in a lift, underspin or topspin dink to force your opponent to make quick decisions on how to handle this varied spin. Your goal is to force an error, not to hit an untouchable winning shot.

Players who relish dinking battles are intimidating. It doesn't take long for opponents to sense this and, if you're a patient dinker, they will either avoid hitting to you or will gamble on ill-advised workarounds, such as speed-ups or lobs. Patiently waiting for the ball to come back high will reward you with an opportunity to be aggressive.

#6: GIVE YOURSELF A MARGIN FOR ERROR

Try to hit drops or dinks 12–18 inches above the net and give yourself a couple of feet when hitting any shot toward the side or baselines. The worst shot in pickleball is a shot into the net. Your opponent will often do you a big favor by hitting a ball that was going out but there's no hope for a shot into the net, so avoid that as much as possible.

Before moving on to low-percentage shots, here are some thoughts about how to handle *short shots*, since they are frequently misplayed. I'm referring to a shot that forces a player to rush forward to hit the ball before it bounces (except on short serves). These balls *must* be dinked. Yes, it's very difficult to move fast-forward and still hit a ball softly, but any other shot either will end as an easy pop-up put away for your opponent or you will hit it out. Don't swing at this ball; just make firm contact and allow your forward momentum to push the ball softly over the net. Running up to hit a ball then hitting it hard could result in you dining on a pickleball-on-rye sandwich! Tell your partner you're going to buy a bulletproof vest and Kevlar helmet if she/he keeps trying to hit short balls hard!

SHOTS TO AVOID

Next, here is my list of low-percentage shots you should rarely hit but probably still too often do:

LOBS

Lobs are difficult to get over opponents and have them land inside a 22-foot court. Anytime your opponents are hitting the ball downward, they are in control. You want to limit your opponents' opportunities to hit in a downward trajectory as much as possible. Unless you hit a great lob, your opponents will likely not only be hitting your high shot down but also hitting it hard at your feet. Don't fall in love with this shot! Far too many intermediate players hit this shot because they have some success against opponents with poor footwork. Pros have great footwork and that's why they rarely lob. It's a very low-percentage shot for them and if you use it too much, it may keep you from climbing the skill-level ladder.

"HERO" SHOTS

These are shots hit when you're pulled out of position and are off balance. When you score with this shot, everyone watching will praise you as a hero. The problem is that these shots don't often work. Attempting to return a great shot with an even-better shot is foolish, a mistake almost everyone makes too often. It's better to respect the excellent shot your opponent hits and just make a return any way you can. I know several very talented 4.5 players who are constantly attempting hero shots. Then they wonder why no one asks them to be their partner in tournaments. Experienced 4.5+ players know they can't win with a partner who gives away points trying to show off and can't trust them to resist trying to be a "hero" on game point.

SIDELINE DRIVES

Unless your opponent creates an unusually large opening that invites you to hit down the line, it's not worth the risk. Hitting down the line turns the sideline into another defender for your opponents. The risk outweighs the reward and makes this a type of semi-hero shot. Intentionally hitting down the line to exploit the weaker side of an opponent *is* a sound strategy, but requires carefully weighing the benefits against the risks of hitting it out or into the higher part of the net. In other words, take the sideline out of the game.

SHORT-ANGLE SHOTS

Any short-angle shot must clear the highest part of the net and quickly drop inside the sideline. One example is a straight-ahead dink angled toward the sideline. Another example is a return of serve hit at an extreme angle toward the sideline. A short-angle shot brings into play both danger zones: the higher net and sideline. This is why it is a low-percentage shot but, again, it's a shot people like to try frequently and yet another shot that wins praise but no medals. I once told a 3.5-level player friend of mine that he would be a 4.0 tomorrow if he stopped trying to make the hardest shots, like this one. Again, take the sideline out of the game.

SPEED UP SHOTS

These days, it's hard to find a patient pickleball player. Social and recreational players try to play almost every shot aggressively, especially the fourth shot. Understanding the "Rule of 3" is a statistically proven model for success in tennis and pickleball. This means that if you are disciplined enough to hit the same shot three times in a row, your opponent will typically take a risk and attempt to change direction.

Rarely will someone hit more than three shots before attempting to end the point with a hard shot directly at the opponent or make an attempt to hit it by them. Speeding up a ball that is higher than the net is a good play but every inch the ball drops below net level becomes more of a gamble. Anytime you hit up on a ball, you're in a defensive position. One of the most common mistakes in pickleball is trying to hit a ball hard from a bad court position (no-man's land, for example) or ball (too low) position. The 4.0+-level players will usually make you pay a price if you attempt to speed up a ball significantly lower than the net, or from a bad court position. The lower the ball drops, the higher the chances are that the ball is going to go out if hit hard. Consider the trajectory a low ball must take to clear the net. The chances for a low ball hit with pace to come down inside the baseline are slim, even for advanced players using heavy topspin. The real challenge is resisting the urge to hit this ball.

THE BEST SHOT IS THE ONE YOU DON'T HIT

Want to win 3-5 more points per game? Stop hitting "out" balls! Most intermediate-level players hit at least this many out balls *per game*! It is irresistible to hit a ball that's within reach. After all, hitting pickleballs is fun and that's why we came to play in the first place, right? Holding back from hitting an out ball takes a great deal of mental discipline and some experience. The ability to quickly recognize a ball is going out is a major separator between levels of play. Professional-level tennis or pickleball players usually know if a ball is going out the second it's struck, and they rarely hit an out ball. Pros are so attuned to this skill that they think a ball that lands two inches outside a line is *way* out.

This keen judgement comes from years of experience. There's no substitute for game experience, but the following tip will give you a load of practical experience quickly. Have a friend hit balls hard at you from all different positions on the court. Don't hit any balls above chest high. Think how a boxer "slips" a punch. Practice ducking and turning your shoulders out of the way. Take note of where the balls are landing. I think you'll be surprised at how many land out. Angled shots are particularly troublesome for inexperienced players to assess due to misjudging where the sideline is. Try to break the habit of wanting to hit anything you can reach.

Here are a couple of pearls of wisdom to help with judgement:

1. "If it's shoulder high, let it fly." A ball hit relatively hard, coming toward you at shoulder height, is likely going out. There are other factors in play such as being with the wind or against it. The amount of top spin your opponent uses to drive a ball must be considered as this causes balls to drop quickly. In general, anyone hitting a ball hard to your shoulder height will find it very difficult to keep in.

2. If you are surprised by a shot, it is probably going out. In other words, if someone should have dinked a low ball but tries to hit it hard, instead, it is most likely going out. Failing to hit a ball that lands in the court is nothing to be ashamed of, though. It actually means that you are a critical-thinking player.

One particular gentleman in my home club, "Al," used to love to step back from the kitchen line and speed up a return with a big forehand drive. He often did well with this tactic, blasting his shot directly at his opponents (including me!), forcing us to hit the shot in protective self-defense. I eventually figured out how to counter this move by watching for him to take that step back. The second he drew his arm back for that big forehand drive, I simply walked off the court! Nine times out of ten, the ball hit the fence. I did this on several consecutive play sessions until Al was forced to adjust. To his credit, Al is now a more patient player.

RETURN OF SERVE ·

There are three types of good service returns: deep, deeper and deepest. Try to get your return to land within four or five feet of the baseline. This should be your goal on *every* return of serve. A deep return of serve makes your opponent's third shot very challenging and makes it much more difficult for them to reach the kitchen line. The speed or spin of your return matters far less than its depth.

In the previous chapter, I recommended that players having trouble with mobility hit a "moon ball" return of serve, since it will give them more time to reach the kitchen line. I highly recommend this return for everyone. I call it a "sucker" shot because opponents see this slow, high ball coming and they are sucked into wanting to crush it. I estimate that players hit this shot into the net or out 80 percent of the time. The moon-ball return is a great tactic to help your game and win you points.

Remember, the key to this return remains the same as with any other return — get it deep! (Failure to keep it deep voids the warranty on this tip.) The reason this slow-motion return is so difficult for players to hit is that they rarely hit a ball that requires them to generate all the pace. The ball also bounces high and out of their normal strike zone. Professional players easily handle this return by slicing the ball down into the kitchen, but you won't be playing against professionals, yet, until you finish reading and following all my advice in this book!

FINISHING SHOTS

The kitchen line is the winning line. Burn that into your permanent memory. Once you arrive at the kitchen line, the real work has just begun. Everything you do here on the court should be trying to get your opponents to hit a weak shot, a shot you can attack. When you get an attackable ball, this is the time to be aggressive. Just like in poker, when you're dealt a pair of aces in the hole, it's time to bet aggressively. Be heartless! I recently had a coronary CT scan done and they found *no* heart! Put away your Mr. Nice Guy or Ms. Congeniality side and transform into a remorseless aggressor! Take out your frustration and whack that ball! It feels great to slam one away. It doesn't matter if you miss one because it was the right shot. On the other hand, there's nothing more deflating than battling an opponent through multiple shots, finally getting him or her to pop one up, and your partner is out of position or hits a Dairy Queen Softy.

EVALUATION

The best way to evaluate your shot selection is by using the chart I created that shows the shots being used and which ones are being missed or need work. I suggest having a member of your playing group do this for you and in exchange, you can chart them.

SHOT	ATTEMPTED	UNFORCED ERRORS
Deep Serve		
Deep Serve Return		
Drop		
Volley		
Dink		
Drive		
Lob		
Overhead		
Shot		
Set-ups		
Winners		

SUMMARIZING

Good shot selection means playing high-percentage pickleball while eliminating low-percentage shots. Winning pickleball is all about being the team that makes fewer errors, not the one hitting more winners. Dave Weinback is the most decorated over-50 professional player on tour. He says that he typically gets applause only twice during a game: occasionally, for hitting a great shot and regularly for ascending the medal stand. Make your opponents take all the risks. When they hit an amazing short-angled shot for a clean winner, applaud them and say, "Great shot!" Then hope they keep trying it! They'll get the applause and you'll get the medal!

The team that hits *downward* the most will always win. The team that hits *upward* the most will always lose. So, think about which shots force your opponents to hit *up*. Underspin (slice) shots are excellent because they stay low and require opponents to hit up. Use topspin drives to exploit an opening. They move faster than slice drives. Sidespin shots can be effective as a change of pace or as a way to get the ball to an opponent's weaker side. One last tip—expect *every* ball to come back!

Think of a traffic light at the no volley line. A ball coming at a height over your waist is a "Green" light to swing away or hit an aggressive shot that either ends the point or puts your opponent in serious trouble. A ball that will reach you somewhere between your waist and knees is a "Yellow" light. Meaning, hit this ball with caution. Do not take a big swing or take too much risk with a ball at this height. A "Red" light should flash in your head to any ball heading below your knees. This is the time to be safe. Admit to yourself that your opponent has hit a very good shot. Just try to get this ball back into the no volley zone. I love this analogy and wish I thought of it but credit this one to Tyson McGuffin.

CHAPTER 10

PARTNER COMMUNICATION

S ince most pickleball is played as doubles, your success as a player will largely be determined by how easily you can mesh with new partners. Doubles pickleball is a team sport. Many less-experienced players attempt to play doubles like "skinny" singles, or with a "This is *my* half and that is *your* half of the court!" mentality. It's common to hear inexperienced players complain about a partner being a "ball hog."

While it may be rude to step in front of someone in a checkout line, or obstruct someone's line of site, in pickleball, stepping in front of a partner is usually a good thing to do, assuming that your partner isn't over-stretching to reach the ball. It simply means that s/he is being aggressive. The sooner a ball can be contacted and returned, the better it is. Making contact with a ball even six inches sooner than a partner does makes a big difference in the quality of the return. Doing this gives your opponents less time to prepare and you often create a better angle for your shot.

This chapter will teach you how to effectively communicate with your partner in all situations. There are two types of teams that communicate very little in pickleball. First, teammates who have been playing together for many months and instinctively know exactly what each other is going to do during play. They know what each other's needs are when faced with adversity. A seasoned team usually has little need to communicate, other than using common on-court directives. The second type of team that rarely communicates has inexperienced players who don't know what to say or who aren't sure *if* they should speak at all. This chapter is for that team.

THE BASICS OF BEING A GOOD PARTNER

Learning what it means to be a good partner is an excellent first step before delving into the contents of effective partner communication. If you're looking for a new partner with whom to play in an upcoming tournament, you should talk with, practice, and play with your prospective teammate first. Finding the perfect partner is more about successfully blending personalities and styles of play, rather than about sheer playing ability. It's similar to dating, there's more to finding a great match than looks, alone.

As with any relationship, building a sound partnership on court takes time. At the core of a good team is trust, built on honest communication. That means that you listen to each other's needs as they're happening and exhibit mutual support through good times (winning) and bad (losing). A smart partner knows what to say and whether or not to say it. Good partners respect the uniqueness of their partners' games and the potential blend of skills they bring to the team. Most importantly, a good partner always has your back on the court, even when what you've done is wrong. Any corrective counsel should be offered in private.

A good partner stays positive and *never* blames a teammate for a loss. Back in 2017, I missed an easy put away at 11-10 on match point. We ended up losing the game, not medaling, and missed out on a cash prize. My partner was distraught and appeared dumbfounded about how I could have missed such an easy shot. His way of blaming me was to give me the passive-aggressive silent treatment. He left the tournament without saying a word and never spoke to me again. Some partner!

Unless you play a perfect, errorless game, you contribute to every loss, at least in some way. The player who hit the final, losing shot should never bear the responsibility for the loss. My "silent" partner seemed to forget all the service returns he netted. Weeks later, I learned that this guy put his name on the tournament's "needs partner" list because no one from his 1,000-member club would play with him because he had a reputation for being a bad partner. *That* was certainly true! The Golden Rule applies here: Treat your partner with the same respect you expect from him or her.

Another characteristic of a good partner is never giving up! *Never quit on your partner or yourself.* Always give 100 percent, out of respect for your teammate. The only safe lead in pickleball comes from an opponent that stops giving maximum effort. A runner always finishes the race. I've seen a player walk off the court in the middle of a game because she realized her partner had given up. She felt humiliated and was totally justified in doing so.

Finally, don't try to coach your partner, or anyone else, for that matter. Most players don't want unsolicited advice and some are offended by it. Instead, ask if you can make a suggestion or if reminders like, "Up to the kitchen line after a service return" are okay. Coaching advice is usually best received well after the match is over. Well-matched partners respect each other's game, enjoy their teammates, and have fun playing together.

TYPES OF COMMUNICATION
PRE-MATCH

If you're playing with a new partner, it's wise to have a conversation to get to know one another. Ask your partner what his or her strengths are and the type of game she/he likes to play. Ask if there's a particular shot she/he would prefer that you take. If she/he's left-handed, ask if she/he prefers to stack. You might also want to know if she/he likes to poach or use hand signals. Of course, you'll want to share *your* preferences, too. Last, be sure to come to an agreement on how to handle down-the-middle shots and an opening strategy for your first game.

ONE-WORD COMMANDS

This is the most common form of partner communication. Use these universal, one-word directives for speed and clarity. Just like military commands, these words must be obeyed without question or hesitation. The following should become part of your on-court vocabulary, in order to play effectively as a team at any level:

- **"Yours"** or **"Go"**: Informs your partner that you want him or her to hit the shot.

- **"Mine"** or **"Me"**: Means that *you* really want to hit this shot and tells your partner to give you space.

- **"Bounce"**: Tells your partner to let the ball land before attempting to hit it because you think it may go out, but you're not sure.

- **"Out"** or **"No"**: Implores your partner not to hit a shot. This is particularly helpful for a partner who struggles with judging whether or not a ball is going out. These words are also used to inform the opposing team that their shot was out of bounds.

- **"Up"** or **"Short"**: Helps a partner anticipate a ball that is going to land significantly short and encourages him or her to move toward the kitchen line.

- **"Switch"**: Informs a partner that you're aggressively attacking a shot on their side of the court and that you intend to stay on that side. This command tells your partner to cover the side of the court you just vacated.

- **"Back"**: Warns that you just hit a shot that's going to be smashed by your opponent. This should allow your partner to retreat and assume a defensive position. This command is usually followed with another single word, "sorry."

- **"Help"**: This is an emergency plea for assistance on a ball you're going to have great difficulty reaching, despite it clearly being your responsibility.

IN-GAME COMMUNICATION

These are brief statements usually related to tactics or a change in strategy. I have a few little phrases that have become a regular part of my on-court vernacular:

- I like to say, "Let's make *them* win this point," as a way of planning to play the next point safer, after gifting the opposition several recent points.

- If I want to encourage my partner to play a softer game I might say, "There's a three-dink minimum at this table (court)."

- When my partner misses a high-risk shot, but I thought it was a good time to go for it, I'll say, "That's okay, good try; it was worth the risk," which implies that I didn't think it was a shot that should be tried without a substantial lead.

If a plan of attack is agreed to, such as refraining from trying to speed things up against a team whose hands are particularly quick, and I stray from the plan for some reason, I may break off a line from Maverick in the original *Top Gun* movie: "I'm *not* leaving my wingman (again)." Hopefully, this will reassure my partner that I'm going to stick with the plan. Of course, encouragement is always something you want to communicate to your partner. I'll discuss this in detail in the "How to Help a Struggling Partner" segment at the end of this chapter.

NON-VERBAL COMMUNICATION

Everyone knows the old axiom, "Actions speak louder than words." This couldn't be more true than on a pickleball court. Your body language says everything to a partner. Eye rolls, shoulder shrugs, deep sighs, turning your back, or throwing up your arms can have a major impact on your partner's confidence and ability to relax. Over long pickleball careers, good partners should have several Academy Awards for Best Supporting Actor on their mantles. *Never let your partner see your disappointment.* There will be times when it seems like your partner can't hit a beach ball back over the net, or when you really want to beat particular opponents but your partner's substandard play kills your plan and you become completely frustrated.

When your partner knows that s/he's stinking up the court, that's when she/he needs your reassurance more than ever. Even a hint of your disappointment can put more pressure on your partner. Fist pumps, claps, smiles, high fives, fist bumps, and paddle taps are the best forms of non-verbal communication. Have you ever noticed that volleyball players always gather around a teammate, even if they just hit a ball into the bottom of the net, or how basketball players will hustle over to encourage a teammate that just "bricked" a free throw? This is how a good pickleball partner should behave, especially if the missed shot is devastatingly costly.

Hand signals are another form of non-verbal communication. The signal comes from the player at the kitchen line to inform his or her partner if s/he intends to switch or poach. Typically, an open fist placed behind the back tells a teammate to run to the opposite side of the court after returning a serve. A closed fist means, 'Stay on that side.' Hand signals can also be used to inform an opposing team if their shot is in or out. A hand held flat, parallel to the court surface, as if pushing toward the ground, indicates that the shot was good. Pointing an index finger up, signals that the shot was out.

POST-GAME COMMUNICATION

In victory, be sure to share the glory. I once had a partner proudly tell me he put away 14 shots in an important tournament game. He didn't say one word about my play and clearly implied that *he* was responsible for the win. This threw a big bucket of cold water on my exuberance. Never do this to your wingman. In defeat, assuming that you plan to play again with this same partner, a discussion on how you both could improve, as a team, might be helpful. Avoid being critical and offer advice only if asked.

HOW TO HELP A STRUGGLING PARTNER

There's no more important time to be an excellent on-court communicator than when your partner is struggling. This is when superior communicators can make the greatest impact on the outcome of a game. Anyone who has been in a relationship knows that it's tough to determine whether to not to say anything to a partner who's upset. Once you realize that your game or match will be lost unless your partner can make a quick turnaround, you must do something to help. The trick is knowing *what and when* to do that something.

Do your best to diagnose the problem. The issue could be focus, dealing with pressure, or simply the need for encouragement during a period of bad play. In the middle of a tournament, I had a partner say to me, "I think this is the worst I've ever played in my life!" I inferred this as a plea for understanding and responded, "I know your talent; you have nothing to prove. Relax! Let me take all the balls up the middle for a while. Your game will come around soon." After the first good shot my partner hit, I put extra emphasis on positive reinforcement with an enthusiastic paddle tap.

Your compliments must be sincere *and specific* in order to be effective. Instead of just saying, "Nice shot!" say, "I like how you took something off and controlled that shot" or "*That's* the way to hit a deep return!" I believe that the encouragement I've given my partners is largely responsible for amazing comeback wins from 2-9 and 2-10 deficits in tournament competition. Telling your partner that a certain part of your game is failing and that you need help is a key example of the direct, honest communication that good partners need to share.

IF YOU BELIEVE THAT YOUR PARTNER IS PLAYING POORLY BECAUSE HE OR SHE IS DISTRACTED OR HAS LOST FOCUS, THEN THERE ARE A FEW THINGS YOU CAN DO:

- Tell him or her to try the deep breathing exercises you learned earlier in this book.
- Help him or her to stay in the moment by asking, "What will win us some points *now?*"
- Avoid talking about why you're losing or why a certain shot isn't working.
- Think about what you *want* to happen, not about what you're *afraid might happen.*
- Set a new, fun goal. Tell your partner, "I'll give you five bucks if you hit the guy in the red shirt."

Another tool to put in your fix-it bag is humor. Well-timed humor is sports medicine. A laugh during a crisis of poor play can be the quickest and best "reset button" for focus that there is. If you know your partner well, she/he might appreciate some sarcasm like, "Wow, if I knew you were gonna play *this* bad, I would've worn a bulletproof vest!" or "I would've taken out a life insurance policy if I knew you were gonna play this bad!" I know a few friends who would respond positively to this type of humor. I've gotten some nice laughs from partners who desperately needed it, with comments like, "Forget those last shots; we're like diarrhea now—on a run!" or "Do you smell that? 'Cause *I* smell *comeback!*" Once your partner returns to normal playing, say, "You're like Campbell's Soup: "Mmm, mmm, good!"

When your partner is playing poorly, a smart opposing team will target him or her. If you notice shots that should be hit to you are all going to your struggling partner, there are several things you can do to change the assault. Call for a timeout and tell you partner that you'll take all the middle-court balls, including overheads. Becoming extra aggressive is another great way to help. Poaching balls at the kitchen line or crossing over to attack a weak return of serve can also be very effective. Even faking a poach will cause your opponents to have second thoughts.

When they're working over your partner with multiple dinks, you can help by "squeezing." That involves moving well past the centerline, which will force your opponents to hit into an increasingly smaller area if they want to keep targeting your struggling partner. This will enable you to pick off more dinks and the space that you leave open will divert your opponents' attention from your partner and lure them into hitting the ball to you.

HOW TO PLAY AS AN UNBALANCED TEAM

Once you become an intermediate-level player, you'll experience being both the much stronger *and* much weaker partner. It's very important to know how to be a good partner in both situations. Many players wrestle with their ego when forced to acknowledge that they're the weaker player. If you want to win, you must put your ego aside and accept your role.

ROLE OF THE WEAKER PLAYER

I have a friend who is a doctor and part-time professional pickleball player. When he has time to play pro tournaments, he often joins forces with a friend who plays on the pro tennis circuit and plays pickleball on the side. My friend, who is an amazing player, tells me that he plays a support role in his doubles partnership. His dominant partner takes all the middle shots, poaches as he sees fit, and squeezes opponents at the kitchen line. My friend concedes his partner's superiority and understands that his role is to keep the ball in play. Dominant players often get the glory of hitting the "kill" shot, but lessor players appreciate being on the winning team and have to realize how important their complementary role is.

When you're lucky enough to be partnered with a much better player, think about your consistency. Keep the points going long enough to give your stronger partner time to poach or speed up a shot. Concentrate on playing high-percentage shots and avoiding undue risks. The best thing you can say to your dominate partner is, "I'll keep it in play so you can put it away." Say a wordless "Thank you!" to a partner who is forcing weak returns your way by soundly putting balls away for winners.

Lesser partners should realize that being the dominant player can be stressful, as well. The added responsibilities that come with being the stronger player and the pressure associated with leading the team to victory can be taxing. Even strong players can become tense and feel the burden of high expectations. Strong partners can also grow weary of "carrying" a partner, and they sometimes find it hard to stay focused if the overall level of play isn't challenging enough.

ROLE OF THE STRONGER PLAYER

All players want to play their best when they get the chance to collaborate with a superior player. It's only natural for lessor players to try too hard to impress. The job of the better players is to anticipate this and keep their partners relaxed. A confident demeanor and a "We got this!" attitude are often enough. A bad error from a strong player can lower the "I have to be perfect" mentality weaker players bring to the game. I often hear lessor partners say, "Sorry!" after missing a shot. My usual response to that is, "Hey, when *I* stop making errors you can apologize; until then, don't worry about it."

It's also the role of the stronger player to evaluate the strengths and weaknesses of the collective team and develop a game plan. Stronger players assume the role of team captain. I like to say, "You hook 'em and I'll fry 'em" to a partner in an unbalanced partnership. This phrase implies two things. First, you want your partner to be patient and consistent, and second, you're going to be the aggressive player and be responsible for ending the point. Beyond this general game plan, positive reinforcement is, by far, the most important ingredient a stronger player can give to a weaker partner. Praise from a strong player can be more powerful than winning is for a lessor player. If you need more perspective on how a strong player should handle a lessor partner, imagine what it would be like to team up with the #1-ranked player in the world!

Sometimes, when two players who usually play secondary roles join forces, both may be reluctant to assume a leadership role and make strategic plans. They may fear that their opinions won't be respected because their weaknesses have, in the past, been covered by stronger partners. This is where clear and direct partner communication becomes critical to cover the pre-match information, mentioned above, and realize an honest evaluation of partners' respective weaknesses. Unfortunately, this rarely happens and the game/match outcome can be a tension-filled drubbing that includes multiple "I thought *you* were going to take that one!" exclamations, a few near collisions, and the inevitable post-match blame game, resulting in an "I hate playing with Joe!" attitude for both players.

WRAPPING THINGS UP

Remember: Doubles is a *team sport*. You, individually, didn't win the game or lose it; you merely contributed to the outcome. Communication is what turns singles into doubles. A partner who can get to and hit any ball before you can is a good teammate to have. Banging paddles together when making a return is not ideal but it means that both players are being aggressive when there's no time to communicate.

Doubles is not about equality; it's about *merging* skills for the shared goal of winning. The bond that comes from having fun and winning matches as a team is the foundation of two of my best friendships. For me, winning in a team sport is far more satisfying that winning in an individual sport. Maybe that will be the same for you, too.

CHAPTER 11

THE POWER OF PRACTICE

Everything in the previous chapters is "low-hanging fruit," countless ways to become a better pickleball player without practicing or expending much effort at all. You don't need to be a talented athlete, just combine your current skills with my instructions and your pickleball game will improve. Guaranteed.

However, if you're the competitive type and winning is important to you, as it is with most of us, the only way to optimize the quality of your shot making and fix those frustrating mechanical flaws is through *practice*. If you truly want to squeeze every drop of potential out of your game, there's no substitute for practice and there's no short cut. Remember, *nothing significant comes easily*, and practice is the price you must pay.

WHAT *IS* PRACTICE?

I know many pickleball players who say that they're "working" on their game during recreational play. This is a fallacy. *You can't fix your game while you play it.* Hitting the shot that you're hoping to improve just a few times per game accomplishes very little. Even in recreational play, players usually do not want to let their partner down by experimenting with new shots. In a practice session, there's no consequence for making errors, as you quickly make dozens of repetitions of the shot you want to add or improve, repeating that shot over and over, hundreds, even thousands, of times over weeks and months.

The purpose of this repetition is to train your brain to create *muscle memory.* Your muscles have to be trained to react exactly the way you want them to without having to think about how to execute a certain shot. In the 1970s, psychologist Noel Burch created a teaching model in which he referred to the ability to perform an effortless, second-nature task as "Unconscious Competency." This should be your goal for every shot in your pickleball arsenal — to be able to produce a high-quality response instinctively, with no complicated thought process.

> **"Practice puts brains in your muscles."**
> — Sam Snead, golf legend

HOW WILL PRACTICE HELP MY GAME?

Once you've achieved your desired level of competency with the shot you've been working on, it'll be much more consistent under pressure and your increased confidence will lift your whole game. You won't be seen making futile jabs at the ball or swinging wildly, and your instinctive execution will make it look simple to others. Friends say that my signature shot is an angled drop volley. Occasionally, someone will ask how I make it look so easy, hoping for a magical tip that will install this shot into their repertoire. My answer isn't a popular one: *practice.* It looks easy because I've hit it thousands of times across decades of tennis and pickleball practice.

Practice will also help you beat your "unbeatables." Maybe they're a little cocky, even arrogant. Sometimes you get close to beating them but fall short and have to endure the dreaded "Nice game!" comment in defeat. Well, the problem is that they *are* better than you and you know that. As those *Saturday Night Live* body builders, Hans and Franz, used to say, "Hear me now and believe me later" — you *can* beat these players! How? *By outworking them on the practice court!* You already have an advantage since arrogant players think they don't need to practice. Make these players' attitudes part of your private motivation for putting in the extra work, which will make serving up some humble pie to them later all the sweeter.

THE BIG QUESTION: HOW MUCH DO I NEED TO PRACTICE?

It depends on how good (what skill level) you want to be and the amount of time, resources, and desire you want to commit. It also depends on how much *un*learning it will take to break your bad habits.

Let's start at the top and work down. By top, I mean wanting to be the best of the best, not just a pickleball professional but the #1 ranked pro! That's most likely an improbable dream, but there are rewards farther down the ladder of goals. One that may be in your mind right now would be to practice enough to beat your current nemesis or to bump up your skill rating to the next level in your club. Maybe you even have goals that lie in between these two.

Numerous studies have probed what elements contribute to greatness and incredible skill in various professions. Is it genetics, opportunity, pure ambition, or a quirk of circumstance? Anders Ericsson, a psychologist at Florida State University, is renowned for his research in performance theory. He uses the term *deliberate practice* as the key to becoming a master of any profession or skill, and has studied top musicians, athletes, doctors, and chess players, among others. His research concludes that *anyone* can master a skill with intense focus, tedious repetition, and immediate feedback. The best are not just "naturals," but have one constant connecting them — they practiced their skill more than others. Ericsson found that those who practiced incessantly, even obsessively, *never* failed to make it to the top ranks of their profession, regardless of circumstances.

Author Malcolm Gladwell furthered this research and concluded that it takes 10,000 hours of practice to master a skill. He coined the term "10,000-hour rule" in his book, *Outliers*. Of course, this number is an approximation. The natural abilities of the person and quality of practice are variables that may cause the amount of practice time to increase or decrease. Gladwell used several examples of famous performers and other elite professionals to prove his hypothesis.

The Beatles and Bill Gates are excellent studies in achieving greatness through practice. Gladwell acknowledges that these men possessed a great deal of talent and were exceptionally lucky to find great practice facilities. The Beatles practiced in English pubs and nightclubs in Hamburg, Germany. Bill Gates began computer programming as an eighth grader, thanks to his forward-thinking prep school that made an agreement with the University of Washington to share computer time. Gladwell was able to find evidence that the Beatles performed approximately 1,200 times and were required to play eight hours per night in Hamburg. All this practice happened before the Beatles produced their greatest albums, *Sgt. Pepper's Lonely Hearts Club Band* and the *White Album*. Bill Gates secured his practice time by sneaking into computer labs, stealing computer time, and mastering programming 30-40 hours a week, for seven years, until he dropped out of Harvard University.

The 10,000-hour rule can also be applied to sports. My childhood dream was to play in the NBA for the Chicago Bulls. But how much practice would it take to master the game of basketball and achieve this goal? Current statistics say that approximately 550,000 boys play basketball in high school across the country. The NBA only drafts 60 players per year, with about 10 of those 60 being international players. This means that a young American boy has about a .009 percent chance of playing in the NBA. It's impossible to document the time that NBA players spent in gyms, parks, and driveways practicing, but I can assure you that it was *at least* 10,000 hours. Now I understand why I didn't make it!

Okay, let's say that you beat the odds and an NBA team drafted you. You beat out several veteran players and made it onto an NBA roster. As an ambitious pro, you set a *new* goal to be the best; you want to be the league MVP! How much more will you need to practice? The late Kobe Bryant was already an all-star player when he set his sights on being the MVP. He stated that he practiced two extra hours a day to achieve this goal. He used this time to shoot 700-1,000 shots a day, even though he was already one of the best scorers in the league! Larry Bird is another great example. He was the NBA's MVP three times and was a career 88.6 percent free-throw shooter. Nevertheless, before *every* game, he shot at least 300 free throws. Pickleball's Tyson McGuffin is a former #1-ranked professional, and on his podcast admitted that he still trains or practices five-to-eight hours a day!

To be clear, I'm *not* saying that you need to practice 10,000 hours! All those whom I've mentioned above have admitted that they were obsessed with their profession and completely focused on achieving their goal to be the best. I understand that you might have zero aspirations to become the best pickleball player in the country and that your goals are likely to be much more modest. My point is that you need to devote *some* time to practice to achieve any goal.

> **"Talent is a pursued interest. Anything that you're willing to practice, you can do."**
> **— Bob Ross, artist and television host**

PRACTICAL PRACTICE

You don't have to have to be totally obsessed and practice for hours every day, like Tyson McGuffin does, to improve your shot mechanics. Friends who have attended McGuffin's camp tell me that he urges all participants to use an 8-to-2 ratio of practice to play. I could not disagree more with this statement. I think this ratio rule will have the opposite effect that Tyson is trying to make, because it is unrealistic to expect amateurs to practice like a full-time professional. It's always better to practice harder instead of longer. *Make maximum use of your practice time.*

Tennis great, Jimmy Connors, believed in practicing for only one hour, after he became a top player. This kept him sharp and decreased wear and tear on his body. His one hour of practice was well planned and very intense. For pickleball, you may be able to go a bit longer, but you don't want to burn yourself out. The process of getting better takes time. Pace yourself for the long haul and have a practice plan before each session. The following suggestions will help you make the most out of your practice time:

GET A PARTNER

Having a great practice partner is ideal, will give you honest feedback, and help you stay motivated. This is why fitness experts also recommend a workout partner. It's also very helpful to see how your shots are working against your partner. A good partner can help you work on your mental game as well. It's okay to fail when practicing with a supportive partner. This is when you should experiment with new shots. Try those shots you saw on a video or that you admire in an opponent. You may discover that you have a knack for angled volleys or lobs.

TRY THE "15-MINUTE FIX"

This is my most realistic and practical practice tip. I realize that finding a practice partner who is available as often as you need him or her can be difficult. Most players have no interest in using some of their available playtime for practice, so start asking players to stay with you an extra 15 minutes after playing. You're both already there, the court is open, they already have their playtime completed, and you need only one player in your group to stay. Instead of standing around complaining about the shot you struggled with that day, work on improving it for fifteen minutes. If you make this a routine every time you play, your practice time and repetitions will add up like compound interest on your savings.

HIT SERVES

The serve is the only shot you can practice alone, assuming that you don't have a ball machine. In tennis, the serve is the most important shot in the game. I used to hit hundreds of tennis serves on my own. I enjoyed the freedom of serving whenever I cared to, as opposed to finding a partner.

I didn't put in 10,000 hours but I'll bet that I hit more serves during my last two years in high school than anyone else did in my state. In the end, I could hit a certain spot on the court using any one of three different types of serves. My serve became the main reason for my success. Without this weapon, I couldn't have played at the Division I level. I take this same approach with pickleball.

The serve is far less important in pickleball than it is in tennis, and originally was meant to be simply a way to put the ball into play. However, perfecting your pickleball serve can pay big dividends. This is where practice is critical. Unlike in tennis, you get only one serve per point in pickleball. Whatever type of serve you're hitting, it should go in 95 percent of the time. If you just won two hard-fought points in doubles, winning the right to serve, don't give up your point with a service error. Once you've mastered consistency, work on placement, keeping your serves landing deep. Next, work on directing your serves deep to your opponents' backhands.

As I did in my tennis game, I hit three types of serves: hard top spin, low slice, and lob. Most players have one serve they rely on and this is perfectly acceptable. My idea is to keep opponents guessing, never letting them get comfortable, keeping them back, and forcing them to use their backhands. As a result, I regularly draw weak returns and sometimes get a "free" point. The #1 cause for service errors is a bad toss. If you're making errors on your serve, I recommend that you try the drop serve. By releasing the ball from the same position every time, the ball should bounce up into your perfect strike zone every time. Solo serving practice is the time to experiment with various types of serves. Chances are that you may accidentally find a new serve with which you can quickly become comfortable and add it to your repertoire.

To get the necessary number of repetitions to assure muscle memory for my various serves, I use a simple practice routine. I set up a net in my driveway! I measure off 44 feet, string up an old sheet as a backstop, and throw down a pizza box for a target. Voilà! An instant practice court. I hit 400-500 serves, 3-4 days a week in the summer. I'll also hit a hopper's worth of serves while waiting to play, and after everyone has left the courts. Granted, I don't have "unconscious competency," since I still have to consciously focus, but my serve is almost automatic, consistently deep, and I can go 10-15 games without a single service error.

BUY A BALL MACHINE

There's no more efficient way to get hundreds of repetitions and build muscle memory than to use a ball machine. Lobster Sports has been making quality ball machines since 1971. They currently offer three models for pickleball. "The Pickle" is easy to move and battery operated. It comes with a remote control and has variable speeds. At $1,200, it's not cheap, but this practice partner is always available and never gets tired. With its 135-ball capacity, you can hit a thousand balls in one practice session. Compare this number to the far fewer repetitions you get when "working on" a particular shot during recreation play. Think what 400 repeated third-shot drops would do for your confidence and game, compared to the six or seven reps spread out over a 20-minute game.

PRACTICE WITH YOUR BRAIN

In Chapter 2, I discussed the effect of visualization on peak performance. You can also use visualization to practice. Mentally rehearsing the fundamentals of shot execution can add to muscle memory. Injured Olympic athletes who were unable to train prior to their events have won medals by mentally rehearsing their specialties. The late NBA legend, Bill Russell, said that he would regularly mentally rehearse his back-to-the-basket moves: two dribbles right, left-foot drop step, spin, gather both feet, power up, and shoot. He said that when he got the ball in this position, he never had to think about what to do. Big Russ possessed "unconscious competency."

I have a friend who is a Major in the U.S. Army Special Forces. He's also an expert marksman, one of the best in all the military and is training to become a Grandmaster shooter. Reaching this level obviously takes years of practice and would put him in the top 1 percent of all shooters in the world. In addition to shooting hundreds of rounds on a live-fire range weekly, he tells me that he "dry-fires" (operates his firearms unloaded) for 20-30 minutes every night before bed. In pickleball terms, this means it is beneficial to dry-fire, or rehearse, your shots in your mind or with your weapon (paddle) in hand.

WHAT TO PRACTICE?

In a word? *Fundamentals.* Strong fundamentals are the foundation of consistent shot making and confidence, plus they're what you rely on when things are not going well. But how do you learn fundamentals? As I said before, the greatest aspect of pickleball is also its worst. Pickleball is so easy to play that most people just ask the person who introduced them to the game a couple questions and take it from there alone. The longer people play without learning the fundamentals, the harder it is to unlearn the bad habits that prevent them from being a better player.

Once a player develops a passion for the game, it's *vital* to get on-court professional instruction. This should be your source for fundamentals. Camps and clinics can be a great source, too, but understand that you won't return home a better player. If a three-day clinic is all it takes to advance a skill level, then everyone would be a star. What a camp or clinic *will* do is introduce you to new techniques and provide you with a personalized improvement plan for you to work on at home.

Beware of people calling themselves teaching pros. Being a fine player does not automatically make you an effective teacher. Look for a PPR or IPTPA-certified professional. It's not rude to ask your prospective instructors about their credentials. Compared to tennis, you'll need far fewer lessons in order to grasp shot-mechanic fundamentals. Online videos can be helpful but, once again, if you could improve simply by watching videos, then everyone would be a 5.0 player! At a minimum, ask very good players in your club for tips. Whatever your source of information, it's worthless unless you intend to practice what you're told.

My hope is that *you* will make the quality decision to learn the fundamentals, now that you're hooked on the game. Remember, it's much harder to unlearn a skill than it is to learn a new one. My friends enjoy social pickleball, but I recommend equipping yourself to play both socially *and* competitively.

> "Practice doesn't make perfect if you are doing it wrong."
> — Frank Sonnenberg, award-winning author

Of course, you need to practice all the shots, but dinks, drops, resets and volley battles represent *80 percent* of the shots made in a typical game. Therefore, these shots should be the centerpiece of your practice plans. This means that all other shots, including drives (groundstrokes), should occupy only 20 percent of your practice time. Volley drills (kitchen line-to-kitchen line) improve your chances of winning hand (volley) battles. A way to make volley drills fun is to use a plastic golf ball or a small rubber ball. After you finish, a pickleball will appear to be the size of a softball! You'll then feel like you can't miss.

HOW TO PRACTICE: MAKE IT FUN!

I know that people don't practice because they think it's boring. This is *not* true. Practice can be as much fun as, and even more satisfying than, playing. How can you do that? Make every drill into a contest. Bond with your partner by attempting to reach certain goals together, such as hitting fifty volleys back and forth without allowing the ball to hit the ground, or by hitting twenty cross-court dinks in a row.

You can compete against your partner by playing a game that works on a specific shot, such as a crosscourt dinking game, where you get one point for a missed dink but two points for successfully attacking a dink, and two points for successfully blocking or resetting an attacked dink. "Skinny singles" uses all the shots of a regular game, but is played on just half the court. Playing a game of two-on-one is great fun, too. The doubles pair must keep all their shots inside whichever court half the single player is on, while the single player can hit all his or her shots into the doubles pair's full court. This sharpens the doubles players' shot placement skills since they have only a half court into which to hit the ball.

Another idea is to challenge your partner to a target-shooting contest. For example, see who can get the most baseline drop shots into the kitchen using one hopper of balls, or who can land the most in a row.

See who can hit a target deep in the court the most times. This is great for serving and returning practice. By the way, playing music while you practice adds another fun element to your session. There are no rules against inverting your paddle to play air-guitar or singing the chorus of a favorite tune after finishing a successful drill. If you want to practice playing under pressure, try adding a "loser buys lunch" element to a contest. Watch the intensity and *fun* ratchet up!

Another way to enjoy practice is to "groove" your strokes. Grooving is another word for hitting the same shot repeatedly, to the point where it feels automatic and you can't miss, even if you swing as hard as you can. I enjoy grooving my groundstrokes in rallies, baseline-to-baseline, even more than playing sometimes. When you get to where you can effortlessly stroke 20 or more balls in a row into one of the service courts, your practice session is complete. You'll have achieved muscle memory and the feeling is exhilarating. It means that your mechanics are smooth and your fundamentals are sound. This is when you should put on Earth, Wind, and Fire's *Let's Groove Tonight* and crank up the stereo on your drive home.

> I attended a Nike basketball coaches clinic in 2004. Several of the all-time great college basketball coaches there said that they make every drill a contest, and it always raises the intensity of their practices. As with exercise, if it isn't fun, you probably won't do it long-term. I'm sure that you'll agree that jogging on a treadmill is a boring way to get a cardio workout. However, if you mix in some fun alternatives, such as hiking, bike riding, or swimming, you're more likely to stick with it. To me, none of these activities is as much fun as a contest with a friend. So, challenge your partner to a contest with your favorite drill and feel *the thrill of the drill!*

When you reach a major practice goal, you need to celebrate as if you had just won a medal! Remember when, in the movie *Rocky III*, Apollo teaches Rocky a new boxing technique, which requires Rocky to dramatically improve his footwork and speed. Rocky struggles mightily, but finally demonstrates his improvement by beating Apollo in a footrace on the beach. The main point here is to make your pickleball progress *fun* for the whole journey. Celebrate progress!

> "It's definitely fun when you're able to translate
> your practice into the game. It's fun, and you know that
> your hard work paid off."
> — Kawhi Leonard, NBA All-Star

WHAT TO EXPECT

Expect that any change you make in your shot mechanics or even a small grip change will feel weird at first. Accept that you always tend to get *worse* before you get better when you make a change. It's that "weird" feeling and inevitable missing of shots that causes players to give up too easily and go back to their problematic, but comfortable, old shot. Resist returning to your comfort zone so that you can improve. It'll take time to unlearn your bad habits and build new muscle memory. Never end a drill on a miss; your last shot should be a positive memory for your muscles and your mind!

Expect to improve, but give any change at least a couple months to succeed. Be patient. Pickleball reminds me of what expert poker players say about learning to play Texas Hold'em. "It takes five minutes to learn but a lifetime to master." Remember: *As your shot making improves, your confidence will likewise improve.* Think of the confidence you gain as a bonus gift for all your hard work. When you're in a big game and your muscles start to tense up and your confidence wanes, your mind will remember all the practice you did and immediately give you a sense of calm assurance. You won't miss that next big shot. Practice will make you *trust your talent.*

As I mentioned earlier, which bears repeating here, the best example I can think of to show you how practice can build confidence and trust is my work with a 105-pound, 69-year-old woman who is talented enough to play pickleball with men one-third her age. Her problem was fear.

Specifically, fear of being hit and hurt by powerful young "banger" players. To remedy this, she and I worked on self-defense, not karate techniques, but volley-defense fundamentals at the kitchen line. She had to unlearn her longtime ready position. The backhand volley is the only shot that can protect your entire body. I instructed her to hold the paddle high and point the leading edge at the 9 o'clock position, as I discussed in Chapter 6, regarding how to defend against a banger. This is the optimal position to defend against shots speeding at your torso or head.

I think she was able to reprogram her mind relatively quickly, since the consequence of failure was physical pain! I decided to try a rather extreme technique to give her the confidence she needed to trust her new skill. I asked her if I could fire balls as hard as I could right at her body and head! She paused for a moment but *reluctantly* agreed! From inside the baseline, I slammed ball after ball at her and she easily blocked them all back, including balls headed directly at her face. Her big smile said it all. She now trusts her new skill 100 percent! This improvement took some time but it was well worth it and her play improved immediately.

While attending an Eagles concert not long ago, the great Joe Walsh rhetorically asked the audience, "Do you think we were good in the 70's? Well, imagine what 40 years of *practice* will do!" He then went off on that amazing guitar intro to "Life in the Fast Lane," a magical moment for the audience and a great comment about the power of practice!

"Practice is everything."
—Pete Carroll, Seattle Seahawks Head Coach

CHAPTER 12

GAMESMANSHIP & TRASH TALK

Gamesmanship is the mental part of all sports and it shouldn't be ignored. It involves practices that are somewhat dubious or improper (but within the rules) in order to try to manipulate an opponent and gain an advantage. The most common purpose of gamesmanship is to break the positive momentum or the current "run" an opponent might be on. Any intentional stoppages of play, such as retying shoelaces, feigning injury, or requesting an unnecessary bathroom break are classic ploys. Another common tactic is the use of timeouts, taken solely to force an opponent to think about a current pressure situation. In football, this is known as "icing the kicker." The goal is to break the kicker's routine and give him time to think about the consequences of missing. Basketball coaches do the same thing when the other team is shooting crucial free throws at the end of a game. By far, though, the most interesting and nefarious form of gamesmanship is the psychological warfare known as "trash talk." Trash talk is language intended to demoralize, intimidate, or taunt opponents.

The best trash talkers of the past were often the very best at their sport. Muhammad Ali may be the GOAT (Greatest Of All Time) of trash talkers from any sport. Ali was as quick-witted as his hand speed. The most clever and creative trash rolled off his tongue effortlessly. As heavyweight champ, he once said, "I'm so mean, I make *medicine* sick!" My personal Ali favorite is, "If you even *dream* about beating me, you better wake up and apologize." Most former NBA players from the 1980s consider Larry

Bird to be the trash-talking GOAT in basketball. "Larry Legend" dished out some great one-liners. For example, prior to the 1986 NBA three-point competition, he declared, "So which one of you is coming in second?" In a holiday mood, he promised, "I don't know what you got for Christmas but I know what *I'm* gonna get you." These classic comments represent trash talk at its best and are designed to put a crimp in the confidence of the opposition.

Gamesmanship is definitely part of pickleball. Since pickleball points seem to come in bunches, anything you can do to break an opponent's rhythm or "run" is a smart move. The strategic use of tournament timeouts is the most legitimate and effective strategy to accomplish this. I recommend using one of your two timeouts per game if the opposing team (or singles opponent) scores three consecutive, unanswered points. Four points in a row should require an *automatic* time out from you. In non-tournament recreational play, you might take your time retrieving the ball, tie your shoes, or have a strategy chat with your partner. Any gambit that can disrupt your opponents' momentum adds points to your pickleball IQ. Pickleball is not immune to *trash talk*, either. I have heard young professional pickleball players observe that the biggest difference between their tour and the senior tour is the amount of trash the senior pros use.

Incorporating a little trash in your game could help you in two ways. First, it's fun, and when you're having fun, you usually play relaxed, and when you're relaxed, you'll play better. Second, well-timed trash can be an effective psychological weapon. The saying, "I'm in his head," means that you have successfully attacked your opponent's psyche. This attack could break an opponent's rhythm, knock him or her out of their zone, or possibly cause a moment of doubt that leads to a loss of confidence. I have experienced a lot of trash talk in my basketball career, but one incident from college tennis stands out.

Our team was at Murray State University in Southwestern Kentucky, a school known for being a tennis powerhouse. My singles opponent was "Hans," a chiseled, blonde German, a Boris Becker lookalike, cut quite the figure and looked like a guy who modeled tennis shirts for *World Tennis Magazine*. He also had quite the female entourage. Just before the start of our match, two beautiful coeds walked by the courts and yelled out a flirtatious, "Hi, Han-sie!" to which he responded in his thick accent, "Girls, don't go! This won't take long!" He was right, and I became his trash-talk victim. Keep in mind — and this is important — there's a fine line between gamesmanship and unsportsmanlike conduct. I'm in no way encouraging unethical behavior to gain an advantage. I take great pride in being called a gentleman on the court and am proud to have won a sportsmanship award in the past.

I usually restrict my trash talk to my regular group of players/friends who can appreciate (or tolerate!) my sense of humor. I don't try to establish residence in my friends' heads or trash it up all the time, and I *never* do it when someone is frustrated and playing poorly. Be warned, though: if you have the audacity to deploy trash talk outside of your regular group, especially at a tournament, be careful! You better have "game" to back it up and be prepared to get a reputation as a major "Jackwagon." If you dish it out, you had better be able to take it. I actually get a big kick out of hearing some friendly "back at ya!" trash talk from my group during recreational play, especially from some of the mild-mannered players I know. *That's* fun.

What follows is a glossary of genuine "fresh smack," as it's known. Your purchase of this book grants you my full permission to "trash" *with care*, as you see fit. I have walked the talk, you might say, and actually uttered or acted out all of the listed expressions at one time or another, although mostly in friendly "rec" play. Think of this list as an *Urban Dictionary* for pickleball. Even if you'll never be a trash-talker, I hope you find something here that will inspire a laugh or two.

TRASH TERMS

The Crucible utterance. "You're in the crucible!" When you're in control of a dinking battle, it's completely against the rules to speak to your opponents while the ball is in play, so say this this only among loose-ruled friends. It's a super-cocky thing to do, but so much fun. I have also declared, "You know, this isn't gonna end well for you!" during dinking battles. Yeah, I'm such a Jackwagon!

The Woodshed. "Pointed to" after beating an opponent 11-2 or worse, as in "pickeling" them (11-0). Walk over to your opponent and ask if they can see "it" in the clearing, through the woods. When they ask what they're supposed to be seeing, tell them you just took them "to the woodshed over there," as you point. A member of my club will say, "Damn, I just got woodshedded!" after losing badly. For those of you not familiar with this expression, in much older times, it was sometimes necessary for misbehaving children to be ordered to the backyard woodshed to get (in today's terminology) a strong application of corporal punishment from their stern, no-nonsense fathers.

The Maxwell. Using your best Don Adams impersonation from the old 1960s comedy, *Get Smart* (younger readers can look this up on their phones), say "Missed it by *that* much!" while giving the one-inch hand signal with your thumb and forefinger, after a ball hits the fence on the fly or otherwise misses the line by a country mile.

FTD Guy. Next time your opponent displays incredibly poor footwork by leaning way over to one side while standing on one foot, ask, "Hey, do you deliver flowers? 'Cause you look just like the FTD (logo) guy."

All You Can Eat. That's what I call unlimited play—a day of pickleball when no one is concerned about time constraints. A pickleball buffet!

TRASH TALK PLOYS

"Who Should I Play With?" When a new player enters a game and asks this question, respond with, "It depends; do you like winning?"

"9-1-1." Whenever you have the chance to announce this score, follow it up by saying that's the number they should call because there's about to be a crime committed: their brutal defeat.

"No Supper!" Said to your partner in a cocky tone after a particularly good win. "We sent them to bed with no Supp-ahh!" This was another parental-discipline tactic from previous generations, but never inflicted on me, thankfully.

"The Timeout" Ask your opponents, "Do you need a time out?" in the midst of your big comeback. Then, just before serving, pause and ask again, "Are you sure?"

"Tie Game Offer" After you've won a couple points in a row, in a game you are losing badly, ask your opponents if they want to call the game a tie. If you win another point, tell them, "This is your last chance," implying that a tie is a much better outcome for them than losing.

"Last Chance." Yell out, "You better win *this* point!" before your opponent serves at 10-9-2, implying that you will win if there is another side out.

"I'll be Home Soon, Dear." After you win the first game of a best-of-three series, tell your opponent that s/he should call his/her wife/husband immediately and tell them that s/he'll be home soon. I got this one from Hans the Man.

"Yardwork." A friend of mine said that he couldn't play too long because of all the yardwork he had to do. I said, "Don't worry; you'll have plenty of time to get that done. This won't take long." Another Han-sie-ism.

"Remote Starter." Prior to serving for the game, ask your opponent, "Do you have a remote starter for your car?" When they say that they do, respond, "Good, you might want to get it warmed up now." Similarly, a player got excited by jumping out to a surprising early lead and said, "If I win this game I'm going home!" to which I replied, "I wouldn't warm up your truck just yet." My self-confidence demoralized that poor guy and I won!

"Hawaii 5-0." Loudly belt out the *Hawaii Five-0* TV show theme song whenever leading 5-0 in a game — "Dadah dah dah daaah daah..." What an irritating thing to do!

"Repeat the Score." Ask your opponent to repeat the score when you're ahead 9 or 10 to nothing. If people are watching, cup your hand to your ear and say loudly, "Say again?" until the irritated reply of, "10 – ZERO – 1" fills the air. I did this in a *tournament* to a particularly arrogant team that deserved it. I saw a couple players on other courts who had to stifle their laughter when they heard me ask twice for the score.

"Do You Have *Any* Points?" Ask this while pretending to know only your own score and appear to be politely asking your opponents for help keeping score.

"An Anakin Moment." Said when a player repeatedly attempts to hit passing shots and you easily slam them away. In *Star Wars: Episode III - Revenge of the Sith*, Obi-Wan Kenobi says to Anakin Skywalker, "Don't try it!" before Anakin attempts an ill-advised attack, which results in Kenobi cutting off Anakin's arm and both legs! When using this trash ploy, keep in mind that pickleball is, after all, a kinder and (hopefully) non-bloody sport!

"Vader Trash." The next time you outplay the person who was nice enough to mentor you and improve your game, tell them, "When I left you, I was but the learner, now *I* am the master!" What an ungrateful thing to say, but, hey, we're talkin' trash here!

"Match Prediction." Have your partner ask you what your prediction is for the match. Be sure that your opponents can overhear your little Q&A. When you answer your partner's query, use your best "Clubber Lang" (Mr. T-like) voice from *Rocky III* and say, "Prediction?...*PAIN!*" If you are really feeling it, add an "I pity the fool" who plays against me!

"The 1099." Ask if your opponents want to play for money. Then say, "Nah, never mind; I don't want to have to claim you guys as a source of income on my tax return." After that, they'll think of you the same way they view the IRS.

"Life Insurance." After smashing an easy pop-up toward the player who didn't hit the shot, kindly say, in your most sincere voice of concern, "I hope you got lots of life insurance when you started playing with that guy."

"Douse Those Flames." After defeating your opponents, tell them that you'll buy them a drink to put out the flames that flared up while they were being torched.

"Polite Trash." The next time your opponent-friend's wife or husband is watching your game, walk over to him or her and politely say (within earshot of your friend), "I think you should leave now." When s/he asks why, express concerned caution with, "Because I don't want you to have to witness the terrible thrashing I'm about to give your beloved." I really like this one!

"The Lesson." The next time you're outplaying your friend tell him or her, "You should be paying me for the lesson I'm giving you," or "Would you like some help with your backhand?"

"The Choke." If your opponent-friend blows an important point or loses the game after having had a big lead, share your automotive knowledge: "You know, your game reminds me of what Detroit invented to make starting cars easier — the automatic choke." That should get him or her revved up.

"Think Again." After you hit a winning put-away shot and your opponent says, "I thought it was going out," come back with, "When *I* hit the ball, think again."

"The Challenge." Pull out a $10 bill and tell your friends you'll give it to the first person who hits five consecutive dinks to you, and they don't even have to win the point. I actually did this to challenge myself and get more balls to come my way. Plus, it's a neat incentive to encourage bangers to soften their game and dink more. It's also a pretty cocky thing to do, so it falls under the category of trash.

"The Bounty." Announce that you'll give $10 to anyone who hits a specific player with the ball at least three times during the day's pickleball session. This is a seemingly nasty thing to do, but it adds an interesting twist to play. Give some thought to selecting the player deserving of this treatment and assure that s/he won't take it as a threat. I got this idea after watching Paul Newman in the classic movie, *Slapshot*, where he put a bounty on the head of Tim McCracken, the "head coach and chief punk of that Syracuse team." This tactic also should enhance the target player's defensive fast-twitch reaction time, so it's not complete trash.

"Any Questions?" Said to the opposing team after a particularly great winning shot. I can't take credit for this one, but since it was the very first piece of trash I ever heard on a pickleball court, I had to include it.

"Sanford and Son." Tell an opponent who wins several points due to the ball hitting then crawling over the top of the net, "That was junk!" followed by, "You guys have so much junk we should call you Sanford and Son," in reference to Fred and Lamont Sanford from the 1970s TV sitcom.

"The Fire Starter." The next time you smack a volley past an opponent who tried to "smoke" one by you. Ask, "Didn't your mother tell you not to play with fire?" Beware, any reference to someone's mother is bound to draw a response.

"The Maître D." When playing a ladder or King of the Court format, kindly direct the losers to their new "table" (lower-echelon court). A very proper sounding, "Right this way, Sir/Maam" will crack up even the most disappointed friend.

NON-VERBAL TRASH

"Nail in the Coffin." Prior to serving to win a game, turn your paddle upside-down, hold it with your weaker hand, make a fist with your dominant hand, and mimic pounding a nail. It's a silent and ruthless move but you better win the point!

"The Finger Wag." This is one of my favorites, ala NBA star, Dikembe Mutombo, who would wag his finger and say, "Unh, nuh, unhhh..." after blocking a shot. Do the same thing when an opponent tries to speed up a return and you blast it back past them for a clean winner. Some also refer to this as "The Babu," in reference to the Pakistani Seinfeld character, whose finger would wag in sync with his admonition, "Jerry Seinfeld, you are a very, very bad man!"

"The Courteous Text." Text your friend prior to playing, saying, "I don't think you should play today." When s/he asks why, say, "Because I got a can of whoop-ass with your name on it!" (a variation on "Foreign Trash," above) or "Because I don't want to humiliate you on the court today" Hey, what are friends for, right?

"The Draper." When your opponents are obviously avoiding you and picking on your partner, look bored and pretend to be smoking a cigarette, like *Mad Men* protagonist, Don Draper, in an unproductive meeting! Guilt them into hitting the ball to you. This is an absolute classic. (Even more effective if you pull out a real cigarette, but we all know that serious pickleballers don't smoke.)

"The Fishing Pole." When your opponent "takes the bait" of your fake poach, upend your paddle, hold it by the face, and pretend to be "casting" with the paddle handle's "fishing pole." Use your other hand to reel 'em in.

"The Gunslinger." After hitting a great shot, blow the "smoke" off the top of your paddle's "muzzle" and mimic holstering your "pistol" at your hip. Even better when done in Texas.

"The Karate Kid." Stand on one leg with both arms extended for your ready position, as you prepare to return your opponent's first serve. You'll strike fear into them (or a good laugh)!

TRASH WITH THE REFEREE

I was getting my butt kicked soundly in a tournament game. When I finally scored a couple of points, the ref called out the score, "Seven – *TWO!*" (with great emphasis on the "TWO"). I stopped my serving routine to say, "Hey, why does your voice sound surprised when you say *my* score?" The ref didn't know whether to spit, smile, or swallow, so he started playing it straight when announcing my score. I praised his new inflection, exclaiming, "Now, *that's* how you call a score!" as I was staging a nice comeback. The banter relaxed me and I actually used it for momentum. My opponent started to wonder if the ref was on my side! The ref got a kick out of my spunk and volunteered to do another of my matches. I actually made a friend on this one! Humor can change things.

MIND GAMES

"The Big Compliment." Give this to your opponent, referring to a specific shot with which they're hurting you. Go into detail about how well they're executing it: "I don't know what you've done to improve your backhand volley, but it's really killing me today!" They may start overusing it or overthinking the mechanics of the shot ("Hmm, yeah. I wonder why I'm doing so much better with that.") and start missing. I've seen this happen.

"The Big Stall." Do something to break the roll your opponent is enjoying. This is an expansion of my earlier comments on gamesmanship. These tactics could include sunblock application, toweling off, shirt change, bathroom breaks, asking the referee a question, making a false foot-fault claim, kitchen-line violation charge, or even faking an injury. Granted, the last three are desperate, underhanded, and borderline unethical things to do. I have never tried them but I have seen them attempted.

"The Push-up/Psych-out." This became a signature moment for me in college. After winning the first set against the #1 seed at the Missouri Valley Conference Tennis Tournament, my coach came over and said, "Close isn't good enough this time." It was as if he banged a gong over my head! He was right; this *was* my time! His words fired me up and turbocharged the adrenalin already surging through my body. I needed an outlet right then and there, so I simply dropped and gave myself 20 (pushups)! When I saw the opposing player and his coach stop talking to turn and stare at me, I added a few clap pushups to *really* make a statement. The looks on their faces said it all. That guy from West Texas State University didn't stand a chance after that! I was 20 years old back then, so this tactic is for all you young ones out there because it's not in my playbook anymore.

"Partner Talk." Do you know that a pickleball court is one-third the size of a tennis court? This means that your opponents are almost never out of earshot. Use this to your advantage when "talking" to your partner by saying things like, "Hit it to the chubby guy's backhand" or "If these guys try to lob, we're gonna crush them." Make sure that your opponents hear this because it's really (obviously) intended for them. You might get them thinking about their backhands or instill enough fear in them to eliminate lobs to your weak overheads. Lately, I have been telling my partner somewhat loudly, "If he hits another drive from the baseline, I want you to smash it as hard as you can." This is a "two-fer" tactic that makes our opponent think about his next baseline shot, while giving my partner confidence in his next volley.

"One man's trash is another man's treasure."

— Author unknown

CHAPTER 13

SOME THOUGHTS & A RANT

Typically, the last chapter in a book like this provides a nice summary of main points. As you know by now, I try hard not to be typical in life or in this book. I want to start with a couple of thoughts about two situations that you will certainly come across in your pickleball journey and can have a major impact on how you handle them mentally. A couple of personal ruminations will follow this, focused on topics with which I am certain you are all familiar. I will conclude the book with my own special type of review, an action plan and some final thoughts. So as legendary Chicago White Sox broadcaster, Ken "Hawk" Harrelson used to say, "Sit back. Relax and strap it down!"

HOME COURT ADVANTAGE

Playing on your home court gives you a significant advantage. The home team wins over 60 percent of regular-season games in all major professional sports. Teams compete all season to gain home court/field for the playoffs. Players know that this sharply increases their chances of winning a championship. In the NBA, for example, statistics show that, over time, 53 of the 74 teams (73 percent) that had home court advantage won the championship. That's impressive.

I'm willing to bet that no high school, college, or professional team *in any sport* has a better record on the road than they do at home, over the long haul. I learned about home field advantage as a young boy, playing sandlot baseball. I knew that the ball would bounce up if a grounder went into the sloped area behind second base, and that the bases we used would slide out from underfoot if not stepped on squarely. If anyone hit the tree down the third-base line, it was an automatic double. Most importantly, I knew where the neighbor's dog liked to do his business, plus, if the ball went over the fence where the angry German Shepard lived, that ball was history!

Your community's pickleball courts likely don't have huge scoreboards, deafening crowd noise, booming marching bands, and crazy mascots like the NBA, MLB, NFL, and NCAA venues have, but pickleball courts are unique. There are distinct advantages to playing at a place that feels like "home." Let's take a look at how to benefit from playing at home and, also, how to offset your opponents' advantages when you're on the road.

ON-COURT ADVANTAGES OF PLAYING AT HOME

Earlier, I described those things that can cause a player to be distracted and lose focus. Those same elements can be home court advantages for players who are familiar with the unique features of their courts. The court surface might be "grittier" if it's newer and "slicker" if older. A gritty surface will grab a ball, amplifying the effects of spin, especially topspin. A smoother (slicker) surface allows the ball to skid, which tends to keep backspin (slice) shots low.

Court cracks, depressions, and even a mild slope can affect the ball's bounce. Home players know where these spots are and how the ball will react when it hits them. Balls that land on boundary lines sometimes react erratically, too, by skidding and not coming up. Close-proximity fencing, light posts, and low-contrast background sight lines all require consideration. Courts located near to noise sources, such as high-traffic roads, train lines, and sports field loudspeakers can annoy and distract visiting players.

NON-COURT-RELATED ADVANTAGES OF PLAYING AT HOME

Pickleball players experience the same advantages of playing at home as pro athletes do. You likely get more and better sleep in your own bed. Your pre-match meals are homemade and prepared exactly as you like them, and you can easily maintain your normal routines. Since you'll be playing in your local community, interested friends can show up to support you, since they don't have to travel far. I remember getting an adrenaline boost when my girlfriend, family, or friends came to watch me at my home college tennis matches.

COUNTERING HOME COURT ADVANTAGE WHEN ON THE ROAD

I wasn't very good at countering the home court advantage of my greatest high school tennis rival, Rodney. Our schools played each other twice every year, once on his home courts and once on mine. I lost six times to him on his home courts, but gave him his two worst defeats when his team came to my school. The second of those two victories was the first time I experienced a peak performance, which I mentioned in chapter 1. The biggest tournament in my region was held at Rodney's school, which accounts for four of those six losses. Once, we played a final at a neutral site. I lost, but it was the closest match we ever played. Today, I look back and understand why I was so successful playing at home and how I could have done much better on the road.

Obviously, I was very comfortable playing at home. Having time for a long warm-up session and not having to stuff my long frame into a cramped school bus seat, even for a short 30-minute road trip, helped me. I also always appreciated any supporters who would drop by to see me play.

I wish that I knew back then what I can tell you now. *Playing away from the comforts of your home court is purely a mental challenge.* You have to accept all the unique factors of an unfamiliar court and *train your brain to believe that this court is the same as the one at home.*

A pickleball court is 22 feet wide and 44 feet long, regardless of where on earth it's located. The net is always (or *should* be) 36 inches high on the sidelines and 34 inches high in the middle. This is all that your brain needs to know. All the distractions, court defects, and environmental factors are the same for both players. Coach Norman Dale (Gene Hackman), in the movie *Hoosiers*, pulled out a tape measure to show his team that the basketball court where they would play their state championship game had the exact same dimensions as their court back home.

The best way to ease your anxieties on the road is to arrive at the unfamiliar courts as early as possible. Try to have an extended warm-up to process any court peculiarities and accept them as a "new normal." Ideally, if you can, arrive the day before your event and try to maintain your normal eating and sleep routines. Schedule time to complete the pre-match preparations I discussed in my peak-performance readiness routine (Chapter 3), just as you would at home. *Try to keep your routines as normal as possible.* College and pro teams follow this strategy since they always plan to arrive at least a day or two before their away games. Countering an opponent's home court advantage means having the mental strength to believe that it makes no difference where you play!

THE MENTAL SIDE OF RALLY SCORING

The debate between traditionalists, who favor retaining the current "side-out" scoring system, and pragmatists, who advocate changing to "rally" scoring, has been raging for years. The rise of televised events and tournaments has turned up the volume of that debate. In rally scoring, a point is scored after every serve, unlike in side-out scoring where, in doubles, for example, if a server's team loses a rally, the ball is merely passed to the opponents' side or to server #2, with no point being scored.

Rally scoring is similar for singles; every server's rally results in a point, either for or against him or her.

Pressure from television networks and tournament directors is the driving force behind this change. Both need better-predictable game times to make their events more profitable. Networks must plan for a specified amount of programming time. Television executives crave drama, and the win-or-lose point consequence of every serve rally in rally scoring is what makes it so appealingly sexy to them. The simplicity of rally scoring also makes it easier for TV audiences to understand, compared to side-out scoring. The Major League Pickleball Tour has recently adopted rally scoring.

Tournament directors must limit the number of entrants because of a finite number of days allotted for play, usually three days for larger tournaments. Long games and weather delays can make tournament directors' lives quite complicated. Recreational players waiting in a "paddle stack" queue will like the swiftness of player rotations, too, since games are completed faster. The USA Pickleball Board of Directors is currently considering approving rally scoring for all sanctioned amateur tournaments. Volleyball, ping pong, badminton, squash, and racquetball all have switched from side-out to rally scoring for various reasons. So, like it or not, rally scoring will soon become the norm of recreational play everywhere.

The mental challenges of rally scoring come from the increased importance of knowing that every point counts. Doubles teams that play two bad service points in side-out scoring, but quickly win their serve back from their opponents without giving up a point, often will say, "Nothing hurt." In rally scoring, *every* miss hurts. This means added pressure and a heightened need for continuous focus from players. Aggressive play will become much riskier and, accordingly, more costly.

Pickleball is a game of "runs," those streaks of points won or lost. Rally scoring is rocket fuel for runs. Two losing rallies from one team, followed by a couple of winning rallies from their opponents and—bada-bing, bada-boom!—a four-point run! Having only one server, instead of two inside-out doubles, and having to announce only two numbers, instead of three in side-out doubles, makes executing runs quicker.

There are also mental advantages with rally scoring. Faster games mean shorter wait times. Time spent waiting for a court to open is never a good thing unless fatigue is a factor and you need a break. Rally scoring will actually help with fatigue in a tournament setting because players aren't subjected to unusually long periods of play. Long breaks between matches make staying focused and "in the zone" much more difficult. Extended downtime also allows muscles to cool and tighten up. Typically, tournament players have only a few minutes to warm up again for their next match and most recreational players do nothing at all to prepare to resume play.

If you're as challenged as I am to keep score, then rally scoring will be a welcome change. I may be the worst scorekeeper in my part of the state, not because I don't know how, obviously, but because I'm so focused on the technical and strategic aspects of my game. I know that being a poor scorekeeper is irritating to players and is somewhat embarrassing to me.

My scorekeeping problems aren't due to an aging memory. I'm merely highly focused on my game, my opponents, and how I'm going to play the next point. Apparently, my brain has relegated scorekeeping to the "distractions" file, similar to those I mention in Chapter 5. The simplicity of winning or losing a point after every rally is something even *my* brain can handle. Relieving the stress of scorekeeping will make concentrating on what's important that much easier.

Most importantly, in my view, rally scoring favors the conservative style of play that I recommend throughout this book. This means that high-risk "bangers" will, like the dinosaurs, slowly become extinct. Hooray!

WARNING: DON'T TRY THIS AT HOME!

Watching professional pickleball on television and YouTube is great for pleasure, but it can be bad for your game. Pros can do things amateurs can't. Your local, recreational game is nothing like the pro game, so don't try to imitate it. For example, pros rarely lob. When pros do lob, it works, because it's a big surprise. You and your friends might lob multiple times in a single game. You might notice pros ripping balls down the line or hitting short-angle shots. They can hit these low-percentage shots because they practice them thousands of times. You probably aren't practicing, and when you try these shots in a game, they go into the bottom of the net. You'll see pros constantly rushing to the kitchen line, and they never seem to get trapped in no-man's land. That's because their partner is a pro, too, and this person hits unattackable third shots 98 percent of the time. *You* can't automatically move forward because your partner is probably hitting an *attackable* third shot 98 percent of the time.

If you *do* watch the pros on TV, there are some good things that you can take away from it. Watch the ready position that the pros always use. Note where the paddle is after *every* shot. Watch how deep every serve and return is. Take note of how often the pros dink and how their footwork flows at the kitchen line. Your group may think that dinking should be done only while warming up. There *are* things that you can do like the pros, but try to be realistic.

PLAYING UP OR PLAYING WELL?

"How can I get better without playing with better players?"

This statement makes me crazy! It made me want to write this book!

Several years ago, I happened to be holding a flyer for a new pickleball clinic when a woman came up to me and uttered this dreadful statement. When I cheerfully blurted out, "I know how!" she was shocked. When I handed her the flyer, she looked at it in disgust and then walked away without a word. I never saw her or any of her friends at the clinic.

I believe that this statement is just an excuse for lower-level players to infiltrate higher-level play. These are players who force pickleball centers to display huge signs requiring specific, *provable* player skill levels for entrance onto certain courts. The problem is that players who desire to "play up" don't want to practice and, as we all *should* know, playing is *not* practicing. This book offers these players an alternative that has nothing to do with practice or with whom you play.

This mistaken belief is misguided for many reasons. First, no magical transfer of ability happens merely from being on the same court with a better player. School students don't learn just by going to class. They have to be engaged learners. Good students ask questions, study, practice solving math problems, while comprehending new information and developing their critical thinking. If playing with better players offers the opportunity to learn by experiencing the differences in play and skills and allows for questions about what it takes to move up, then playing with better players *can* be beneficial.

However, most players that do get the opportunity to play with better players don't ask questions and rarely comprehend the differences in play, or note the deficiencies in their own game that are exposed by better players. They don't seem to grasp the fact that simply hitting a ball hard at a good player is no longer a successful tactic, or that they can no longer get away with hitting short returns of serve. The "wanna be" players seem oblivious to skill level differences, or they merely walk away, making excuses about their shortcomings. I've observed many players leaving higher-level courts without a care in world, smiling unwittingly, after losing *every single game*, rotating among multiple superior partners. This person is not going to improve by playing with better players.

Jumping up a level without the requisite skills won't help your game and it could even hurt it. Taking a regular beating and disappointing various partners is not good for anyone's mental health. Losing confidence and becoming demoralized is not going to help your game. You must have complete confidence in the fundamental skills outlined in the ITPF rating system for your level before considering moving up. Skipping a level is detrimental to your development as a player. Remember: *When you're winning three out of four games at your current level,* **then** *think about moving up.*

Players making the "How can I get better...?" statement remind me of my days as an instructor at the World Class Tennis Academy. The most difficult shot to learn in tennis is the serve. My teenaged campers apparently found that learning the fundamentals of serving was too boring. They would tolerate learning how to hit advanced serves, like the slice, but they really wanted to skip the whole natural progression of skill building and jump straight to the most difficult shot in tennis: the American Twist serve. "That would be so cool!" they'd say. This is a serve few college players have mastered, but that's what those kids wanted. The analogy would be like taking on calculus before mastering algebra. Learn to walk before you run!

Congratulations! With that, you've reached the end of my graduate-level course on pickleball wisdom and my special review. As a retired teacher, I instinctively want to write tests after filling my students' heads with information. I know, "No one said anything about a test!" No worries. It's only 25 questions and I'm not giving letter grades. My grades range from praise to sarcasm. If you don't want to be my next trash-talk victim, then study up and do your best!

▶ PICKLEBALL POP QUIZ

Directions: Circle the letter of the best answer. You'll need a piece of paper or you can circle the letter right here in the book, since it is *your* book. The answer key follows the last question. *No cheating!*

1. WHICH TWO THINGS ARE MOST ESSENTIAL TO BECOMING A BETTER PICKLEBALL PLAYER?

a. Goals and plans

b. Shoes and paddles

c. Confidence and clothes

d. Visualization and sleep

2. HOW SHOULD YOU DETERMINE WHEN IT'S APPROPRIATE TO TRY TO PLAY AT THE NEXT-HIGHER LEVEL IN YOUR CLUB?

a. Whenever you feel like it. It's a free country!

b. When you're winning 75 percent of the games at your current level.

c. When your best friend tells you that it's okay.

d. When you think the higher-level group is short a player.

3. THE KEY TO UNDERSTANDING PEAK PERFORMANCE IS:

a. Preparation

b. Confidence

c. Visualization

d. Fitness

4. WHAT DO PLAYERS CALL IT WHEN THEY ARE NARROWLY FOCUSED AND PLAYING THEIR BEST?

a. The Zen Zone

b. In the Zone

c. Hocus Focus

d. My Happy Place

5. WHICH OF THESE SHOULD YOU DO THE MORNING OF A BIG TOURNAMENT?

a. Smoke at least four cigarettes.

b. Have a Bloody Mary with extra hot sauce and pickle juice.

c. Do a full stretching routine.

d. Pound down a hearty breakfast of biscuits and gravy.

6. WHICH OF FOLLOWING SHOULD YOU *NOT* DO THE NIGHT BEFORE A BIG TOURNAMENT?

a. Party like it's 1999.

b. Organize all your equipment.

c. Get an extra hour of sleep.

d. Do a "carb load."

7. WHAT ARE ALMOST ALL AMATEUR PICKLEBALL PLAYERS RIDICULOUSLY BAD AT DOING?

a. Warming up

b. Third-shot drops

c. Lobbing

d. Keeping score

8. WHICH OF THE FOLLOWING SHOULD *NOT* BE IN YOUR PICKLEBALL BAG?

a. A backup paddle

b. Extra clothing

c. A bottle of red wine

d. Food and water

9. WITH WHICH OF THE FOLLOWING ISSUES CAN DEEP-BREATHING EXERCISES HELP?

a. Relaxation

b. Focus

c. Relieving stress

d. All of the above

10. WHICH TECHNIQUE IS EXCELLENT FOR TRAINING YOUR BRAIN TO IMPROVE YOUR FOCUS?

a. Tapping

b. Deep breathing

c. Yoga

d. All of the above

11. WHAT SHOULD A SMART DOUBLES TEAM DO WHEN THEY ARE BEING SOUNDLY BEATEN?

a. Stick to the game plan.

b. Admit that today wasn't their day.

c. Develop a new strategy.

d. Hope their opponents become injured.

12. WHICH IS *NOT* A GOOD STRATEGY TO USE TO BEAT A "BANGER"?

a. Dink more.

b. Match power with power.

c. Get low and block balls back.

d. Let balls go out.

13. WHICH IS TRUE ABOUT MENTAL TOUGHNESS?

a. It's built by overcoming adversity.

b. It's something you're born with.

c. It's something you can learn from a book.

d. It's a benefit of a high-fiber diet.

14. WHICH IS *NOT* A TECHNIQUE FOR OVERCOMING PLAYING UNDER PRESSURE?

a. On court rituals

b. Deep-breathing exercises

c. Staying in the moment

d. Drinking soothing black tea

15. WHAT IS THE NAME OF THE PLACE WHERE YOU ALWAYS WANT TO BE ON A PICKLEBALL COURT?

a. Margaritaville

b. The kitchen line

c. The baseline

d. No-man's land

16. A GREAT TACTIC FOR ALL PLAYERS, BUT ESPECIALLY THOSE WITH MOBILITY ISSUES, IS TO:

a. Call frequent time outs.

b. Hit high-floating returns of serves.

c. Drive the ball down the line for clean winners.

d. Drink multiple energy drinks prior to playing.

17. WHICH OF THESE SHOTS SHOULD YOU BE HITTING A LOT LESS FREQUENTLY?

a. Sideline drives

b. Lobs

c. Short angles

d. All of the above

18. WHEN MOVING FORWARD OR BACKWARD ON THE COURT, WHAT SHOULD YOU DO JUST BEFORE AN OPPONENT STRIKES THE BALL?

a. Split-step.

b. Duck!

c. Pray it goes out.

d. Yell, "Yours!" to your partner.

19. THE BEST AND EASIEST POINT TO SCORE IN PICKLEBALL COMES FROM:

    a. Any shot hit cross-court.

    b. A non-attackable drop.

    c. A dink.

    d. A ball you don't hit that is going out.

20. WHICH IS *NOT* AN EFFECTIVE WAY TO HELP A STRUGGLING PARTNER?

    a. Give specific compliments.

    b. Take all the balls in the middle.

    c. Let out a deep sigh.

    d. Make him or her laugh.

21. THE BEST THING A WEAKER PLAYER CAN SAY TO A DOMINANT, STRONGER PARTNER IS:

    a. "Thank you for playing with me."

    b. "Beware. I've been popping it up a lot lately."

    c. "I'll keep it in play so you can put it away."

    d. "I'm playing much better; over *half* of my serves go in now!"

22. WHICH IS *NOT* A STRATEGY TO COUNTER THE HOME COURT ADVANTAGE?

    a. Practice on an identical court well in advance.

    b. Maintain your normal routines on the road.

    c. Convince yourself that the court is exactly the same as at home.

    d. Arrive early to become acclimated to the courts.

23. THE GOAL OF COMPLETING COUNTLESS REPETITIONS IN PRACTICE IS TO BUILD:

a. Mental toughness and calluses on your hands.

b. Endurance and physical fitness.

c. Muscle memory and "unconscious consistency."

d. A strong competitive attitude.

24. WHAT IS THE BEST THING YOU CAN DO TO IMPROVE YOUR SHOT MECHANICS?

a. Practice.

b. Watch YouTube pickleball videos.

c. Buy a great paddle.

d. None of the above.

25. WHICH IS *NOT* TRUE ABOUT TRASH-TALKING IN PICKLEBALL?

a. It should be used with great discretion.

b. It is strictly forbidden in tournament play.

c. It can be an effective psychological weapon on opponents.

d. It can counter an opponent's trash talk.

BONUS QUESTION: WHICH STATEMENT DO YOU FIND MOST TRUE ABOUT THIS BOOK AND THE AUTHOR?

a. I never imagined there were this many ways to be a better pickleball player.

b. The author is not only brilliant but also incredibly handsome, as well.

c. The book is junk and the author is an egotistical, sarcastic "Jackwagon."

d. Both a and b. (Hint: It's this one.)

ANSWER KEY

1. a	14. d
2. b	15. b
3. c	16. b
4. b	17. d
5. c	18. a
6. d	19. d
7. a	20. c
8. c	21. c
9. d	22. a
10. d	23. c
11. c	24. a
12. b	25. b
13. a	

GRADING SCALE

How many questions did you get right?

25-23: I'll be seeing you on the Pickleball Channel and will expect a shout-out!

22-20: You're ready to impress your friends with your new knowledge and game!

19-17: Time to reread select chapters. I can only explain it to you; I can't *understand* it for you.

16-14: Easy now. Don't let your brains go to your head.

13 or fewer: Never tell anyone you read my book.

▶ FINAL THOUGHTS

I want my readers to know that I actually do everything I suggest in this book, but I'm *not* great at doing it all. Much of what I relate is the result of my mistakes and failures over time, my trials and errors. I hope that you can avoid most of my disappointments by following the instruction and advice across these pages. The process of writing this book has been a big help to my game. It forced me to re-evaluate my approach to pickleball and made me "walk the walk." I've made changes in how I deal with periods of poor play and how to be a more positive force when my doubles partner is struggling. Focusing on my footwork whenever my play declines has been a big help, and I've seen how much finesse and intelligent play can be a dominant force in a pickleball game.

These are just a few of the changes that this book has compelled me to make. I've even become a bit paranoid about being caught *not* doing something I recommend to all of you. Obviously, I don't anticipate that you'll follow *every* piece of advice that I offer. However, if you pick out just a handful of tips to implement, your game will be that much better for it. If you do most of the things I suggest, including dedicating some time to practice, there's a 100 percent chance that you'll be a *much* better player and playing better is simply more FUN! I hope that you'll develop a sense of deservedness after you've achieved your pickleball goal(s). You deserve to call yourself an athlete and an accomplished player.

"There are no secrets to success. It is the result of preparation,
hard work, and learning from failure."
— Colin Powell, General and Former Secretary of State

I have one final goal. That would be for you, the reader, to see me somewhere one day, perhaps on an adjacent court or at a tournament or clinic, and address me with a famous line from the movie, *Patton*. In that film, after General Patton defeats military expert, author, and German Field Marshal Erwin Rommel's troops in a critical tank battle, Patton surveys his victory and proclaims, "Rommel, you magnificent bastard, I read your book!"

Rommel's book was about the art of tank warfare. My book is about the art of pickleball warfare. Thus, after you've surveyed your many battle victories on court, and you encounter me, wherever, don't hesitate for a second to walk up boldly to me, look me straight in the eye, and exclaim, "Satka, you magnificent bastard, I READ YOUR BOOK!" If that ever happens, then my life will be complete!

> "Every year you should be surprised by how
> much better you are."
> — David R. Satka, author and pickleball warfare expert

► ACKNOWLEDGEMENTS

To Dave Berry, of Altoona, Pennsylvania, who encouraged me to write this book, guided me and inspired me to keep going. Dave finally retired well past the typical age but decided that critiquing my manuscript, serving as my writing mentor, and lending me his wordsmith talent was a priority in his budget of "time I have left" in life. I am honored to be the recipient of Dave's most precious gifts, his time, and an unwavering belief in me. Dave used countless tools from his vast experiences to squeeze every last drop of pickleball "juice" out of me and I could not be more appreciative. By far, the greatest gift pickleball has given me is many new friends. I am grateful to have met them all but especially, Mr. Dave Berry. Thank you, Lt. Commander Dave, I could not have done it without you!

To Dallas "Big D" Kelsey III, my college tennis partner who would go on to become the #1 singles player at Indiana State University and is currently Director of Tennis for the Terre Haute Tennis and Pickleball Club and Terre Haute Tennis Association. Thanks for sharing your decades of tennis experience and helping me proofread my manuscript, but mostly for being there for me at every turn in life since we met.

Special thanks to my fellow members of the Blair County Pickleball Club who unwittingly became the inspiration for dozens of topics I would cover in this book.

ABOUT THE AUTHOR

Dave Satka has been competing as an athlete since childhood. He was born and raised in Northwest Indiana where he played baseball, basketball, and tennis in high school. Upon graduation, Dave walked on to the men's tennis team at Division I Indiana State University in Terre Haute, Indiana. He became a four-year letter winner, earning a scholarship on his way to obtaining his Bachelor's and Master's Degrees. Dave began his instructing career at the World Class Tennis Camp in Baltimore and continued as an assistant tennis professional in Altoona, PA. He started his career by serving eight years as an officer in the U.S. Army Reserve and as an administrator in the Federal Bureau of Prisons. Dave followed his passion for teaching by returning to college to gain certification to teach high school social studies. He recently retired after 25 years of teaching history and as an adjunct professor of criminal justice. He was also a successful head basketball and assistant tennis coach during his tenure as an educator.

In 2017, Dave discovered pickleball. He was named USA Pickleball Association Ambassador for Central Pennsylvania and founded the first outdoor pickleball courts in Altoona. Since then, interest and the number of players in the area has exploded. Dave is a 4.5 skill-level player, an advocate for Selkirk Inc., and a Professional Pickleball Registry (PPR) Certified Coach. Dave resides in a small town just south of Altoona. For more information, visit www.winningpickleballnow.com.

▶ SELECTED BIBLIOGRAPHY

Afremow, J. (2013). *The Champion's Mind: How Great Athletes Think, Train and Thrive*. New York: Rodale.

Gallwey, W. T. (1974). *The Inner Game of Tennis*. New York: Bantam Books.

Gladwell, M. (2008). *Outliers*. New York: Little, Brown and Company.